THE LIFE JESUS MADE POSSIBLE

What people are saying about
The Life Jesus Made Possible

"This is an intensely practical and applicable book that helps Christians activate their God-given agency by seeing where God is at work and joining him in His quest to transform the world, inch-by-inch, in the context of everyday life. Dynamic!"

Alan Hirsch
Author & Activist
alanhirsch.org

"Most of us in the North American Church never grab hold of all that God has for us as his sons and daughters. We settle for an insipid, sterile spirituality that lacks any resemblance to the powerful movement of God we see in the pages of the New Testament. This volume graciously challenges us to step up and into our calling. A must read for anyone serious about following Jesus wholeheartedly."

Dr. Sam Metcalf
President, CRM-US
Author of *Beyond the Local Church*

"Thank God for leaders and practitioners like Bill Randall who show us what it looks like to accept God's invitation in joining the redemptive mission of Jesus in the world! 'The Life Jesus Made Possible,' will embolden you to take up your call as an apprentice of Jesus in his magnificent Kingdom and find yourself transformed by the Spirit along the way. A must read for everyday missional people."

Christiana Rice
Coach and trainer with Thresholds
Co-author of *To Alter Your World*

"This book is a must read for anyone who wants to grow up in their faith. Bill will help you understand and integrate the deeper things of God including; the Kingdom, real discipleship, healing ministry and spiritual disciplines."

Dr. Steve Ogne

Author of *The Leadership Ladder* and *TransforMissional Coaching*

"*The Life Jesus Made Possible* is just what we pastors need, and just when we need it. Bill Randall gives us a timely reminder that Jesus never meant for us to follow him and to do "greater works than these" on our own strength alone or all on our own. With a solid biblical and theological background and drawing on years of front-line ministry experience, he demonstrates how community and ministry flows from a vibrant and dynamic relationship with the risen Lord Jesus. And he shows us how being united with Christ clothed with his gospel can shift us from a reactive posture to the world into a proactive, initiating and creative approach toward the world. There is a select group of books that work on the reader like a well-guided retreat, *The Life Jesus Made Possible* is one of them."

Dr. Robb Redman

Founding Dean and Professor
College of Theology, South University

"I am a Millennial. And I lead a movement that's passionate to see Millennials raised up for Kingdom change around the world. They say Millennials are changing the face of culture, faith and the church and have incredible influence on the world today. But Bill's book brings to light essential truths that my generation cannot miss. The truth that only a Spirit-empowered life leads to any lasting impact; The hope that true healing is found in and from Jesus Christ; The challenge of what it means to be a true follower of Christ in today's culture. What Bill articulates in this book is essential for Millennials – and every generation – to grasp if we honestly desire to live with meaning for the Kingdom of God!"

Ben Stewart

Executive Director of Uncharted International

"Bill Randall has been discipling people for well over 30 years and his many years of ministry experience is clearly seen in this book. In an easy-to-read style and blending of personal spiritual formation and discipleship, *The Life Jesus Made Possible* provides solid tools for the reader to equip others to advance God's Kingdom."

Dr. Wanda Walborn
Director of Spiritual Formation, Nyack College, Nyack, New York

"I have just finished reading Bill Randall's new book, *The Life Jesus Made Possible*. I have known Bill for nearly 30 years and this book is a faithful witness to his life and ministry. Jesus Christ is exalted and glorified with great passion in these pages as He has been throughout Bill's life. In this book, Bill crystallizes the Kingdom principles that have centered him on Christ all these years. I recommend it highly to anyone hungry for more of Jesus and His ways."

Dr. Ron Walborn
Dean, Alliance Theological Seminary

"In *The Life Jesus Made Possible*, Bill offers a refreshing look at discipleship. The Kingdom principles he addresses are provocative, but balanced. And most importantly, Bill lives the truths he writes about every day. I heartily recommend this book."

Dr. Rick Sessoms
Founder / President, Freedom to Lead International
Author of *Leading with Story: Cultivating Christ-centered Leaders in a Storycentric Generation*

"From the beginning of this book, I was jolted by the bold assertion that God's Kingdom has *everything to do with everything!*" And I wasn't disappointed as each page unfolded more and deeper truths explaining how the supernatural life can be an everyday occurrence for all sincere followers of Christ. Get ready to be introduced to a reality so rich with God's presence, power, and provision that you'll find yourself yearning to see the stuff of heaven become the substance of earth! I'm hoping this is only the first of many resources we see from Dr. Bill Randall!"

Dr. Myra Perrine
LIFE Coach, Teacher, & People Developer
Author of *What's Your God Language?* and *Becoming One.*

"Many Christians believe God is present in the world today. Bill Randall is challenging us to go beyond belief to actively engage, announce, and advance the Kingdom of God, moving the gospel message from the 'then and there' to the 'here and now'. A must read for those interested in embracing the 'Christ-like instinct to respond to such things as sickness and bondage with expectant prayer.'"

Dr. Terry Wardle
President, Healing Care Ministries
Author of 15 books including *Healing Care, Healing Prayer*

Here is a masterful invitation to a bigger life. To a life of kingdom partnership, power, and impact. It is indeed *the life Jesus made possible*, but it is more. This is the life we were made for. The life we long for. The irresistible life that a lost world -- and in many places, the church -- doesn't even know is possible. Bill unpacks that life in an accessible and thought-provoking way. The Spirit of God is on the move in fresh bold ways in our day and *The Life Jesus Made Possible* invites us to participate in that movement. Thank you, Bill. I will be using this book with leaders I serve around the world.

Gary Mayes, D.Min
Author of *DNA of a Revolution*
Executive Director of ChurchNEXT at CRM

"In *The Life Jesus Made Possible*, Dr. Bill Randall de-mystifies discipleship, the Kingdom of God, and the disciplines of the Christian life. Simply and clearly, he explains how to live out what it means to be a disciple under the reign and rule of God. He stirs us to experience the power of Kingdom discipleship and brings the depth of the spiritual life within reach for every believer. I encourage you to read this book and embrace this life that Jesus made possible."

Paul L. King, D.Min., Th.D.

Author, professor, pastor, Doctor of Ministry mentor, Leadership Training Consultant

Bill Randall's powerful new book is the latest addition to the critical few books which have shaped my life—penned by practitioners deeply entrenched in the crucible of cross-cultural church and mission. Bill captures our attention when he observes *"that people most often lack fascination for God's Kingdom, along with having little desire to organize their lives around it, simply because they've never really encountered it."* Each chapter invites the reader to encounter Jesus, and then equips them to embrace the practices revealed in Scripture designed to fuel a fruitful abiding life with Christ. This is the most theologically satisfying book linking the Kingdom of God, discipleship, spiritual formation, the power of the Spirit, healing, and the mission of the church I have read in decades. (126) This is a book for disciples who want to experience transformation beyond mere knowledge, pastors who want to equip and release disciples for supernatural ministry, and cross-cultural workers desiring to scaffold their discipleship by Kingdom truths and supernatural power, not by formulaic discipleship programs.

Dr. Steve Hoke

Leader Development Specialist, Church Resource Ministries
Author of *Global Mission Handbook: A Guide for Crosscultural Service*
and *Send Me! Your Journey to the Nations*

"Bill Randall's powerful new book, *The Life Jesus Made Possible*, unearths the real meaning of the normal Christian life and teaches us how to walk in our divine mandate as world changers and history makers. This book is a clarion call to all Believers to raise up powerful, supernatural wonder-working Jesus people, and to make disciples of all nations. It's very possible that Bill Randall's book could equip you to fulfill your divine destiny. Whether you're a high-maintenance, low-impact believer living a boring Christian life, or you are a mature leader looking for tools to empower your followers, this book is for you!"

Kris Vallotton

Senior Associate Leader, Bethel Church, Redding, CA

Co-Founder of Bethel School of Supernatural Ministry

Author of ten books including, *The Supernatural Ways of Royalty* and *Spirit Wars.*

THE LIFE JESUS MADE POSSIBLE

Embracing the Kingdom Within Our Reach

BY

BILL RANDALL

The Life Jesus Made Possible
© 2018 Bill Randall

ISBN-13: 978-1493717231
ISBN-10: 1493717235

First edition: April 2018
Cover design by Angie Alaya
Interior art by Mitch Santala

LONG WAKE
Leaving a Lasting Imprint

www.longwake.com

Lasting influence flows from the integration of who we are and what we do as followers of Jesus under the influence of the Holy Spirit. Long Wake Publishing produces resources committed to both.

P 20 19 18 17 16 15 14 13 12 11 10 9 8 7 6 5 4 3 2 1
Y 34 33 32 31 30 29 28 27 26 25 24 23 22 21 20 19 18

DEDICATION AND THANKS

After several decades of teaching, writing and living into the material covered in this book, there is no question that my wife Jill is to be applauded for sustaining her gracious posture of encouragement for me to finish this book. No doubt I have been cheered on by others, but no one has asked me more often than she, "Are you going to write today?" The stories of our life weave in and out of the pages of this book. I am so grateful for you, Jill. You are a remarkable daughter of the King and my best friend. I dedicate this book to you.

Myra Perrine is a friend and mentor who encouraged me and held me accountable at times when I needed it most. In her tenacious style, she often kicked me in the butt when I needed it, but also frequently spoke words that awakened my faith to keep writing. Thank you, Myra.

My previous team and many friends at Risen King Community Church provided a consistent stream of encouragement for me to write down what we were experiencing as a community of Christ-followers. More recently, I have gratefully experienced the prayerful support of my ChurchNEXT Lead Team community to finally publish this book. Thank you all!

I also want to mention a few of those who have impacted me deeply in terms of my spiritual and theological formation. These include Don Williams, John Wimber, Henri Nouwen, Terry Wardle, Archibald Hart, Alan Hirsch and Dallas Willard. It will be easy to discern the influence of these giants on the pages that follow for anyone who has known them.

Finally, thank you Jesus. Somehow, by grace, may this book bring you honor and serve to open the way for many to embrace the life you made possible.

TABLE OF CONTENTS

INTRODUCTION 17
    WHAT TO EXPECT FROM THIS BOOK 20
    WHY THIS BOOK IS IMPORTANT 23

PART 1 THE MINISTRY JESUS MADE POSSIBLE 25
    CHAPTER 1 THE KINGDOM WITHIN OUR REACH.................27
        Making Space for God's Kingdom..........................33
        Other Gospels..36
        The Need for a Leadership Revolution.....................42
        Conclusion...46
    CHAPTER 2 DISCIPLES OF THE RISEN KING..................49
        What is a disciple? 51
        What is discipleship? 53
        The Abiding Life of a Fruitful Disciple 59
        The commitments that support an abiding life:...........62
        The Promise of Power!...................................64
        Conclusion...66
    CHAPTER 3 EMPOWERED BY THE SPIRIT 67
        Reaching A City for God 68
        The Holy Spirit In and Upon You!........................71
        What About Speaking in Tongues? 73
        There Must Be More!.....................................74
        Revive Us Again, Lord! 77
        Seeking His Kingdom First!..............................78
        Truth AND Power: We Don't Have to Choose! 80
        Conclusion...83

PART 2 THE WHOLENESS JESUS MADE POSSIBLE......85
    CHAPTER 4 PHYSICAL HEALING TODAY 87
        God's Desire to Heal 88
        By Grace we are Healed 88
        Conditions Conducive to Divine Healing..................90
        Common Questions Regarding Healing......................98

Healing and Discipleship 103
How to minister to the sick 105
Conclusion 111

CHAPTER 5 HEALING FOR THE BROKEN HEARTED 113
God Desires and Provides for Our Holistic Healing 114
How the Truth Sets Us Free 116
Common Obstacles to Our Emotional Well-Being 119
Conclusion 136

CHAPTER 6 WELCOME TO THE WAR! 137
Jesus Came to Set Us Free! 138
The Foundation for Victory in Spiritual Warfare 140
Can a Christian Be Demonized? 144
Footholds for the Enemy 145
Renouncing the Occult and Idolatry 148
Setting the Captive Free 152
Persevering through a Difficult Deliverance 154
Praying on the Armor of God 155
Conclusion 160

PART 3 THE COMMUNITY JESUS MADE POSSIBLE 161
CHAPTER 7 MAKING SPACE FOR GOD 163
Embracing the Life Jesus Made Possible 165
Following Jesus' Example 165
Practicing the Presence of God 166
Come as You Are 168
Power, Spiritual Formation, and the Supernatural Life 171
The Spiritual Habits 173
The Danger of Legalism 183
Grace Is Not Opposed To Effort 186
Abiding with God All Day Long 188
Conclusion 190

CHAPTER 8 MAKING SPACE FOR FRIENDS 191
What Is Christian Community? 196
The Community Within Our Reach 196
The Purpose of Community 199
Lessons From The Monastery 203

Critical Issues within Community.................................206
Community: The Fellowship of the Imperfect..........................209
Conclusion..210

FINAL ENCOURAGEMENTS 213
WHERE WE HAVE BEEN… 214
WHERE DO WE GO FROM HERE? 217

ABOUT THE AUTHOR 219

WHAT IS PIONEERING INITIATIVES? 220
Could Pioneering Initiatives be a fit for you?...........................222

INTRODUCTION

"There must be more!"

This was the relentless thought I had as I worked my way through my first semester of seminary. The more I studied the Scriptures and considered how God had dealt with his people through redemptive history, the more my heart ached to encounter the reality of God's love and power as others had.

This desperation led me to seek the Lord as never before. For months I would arise hours early before classes to read and meditate on Scripture and cry out to God. Finally, on the last day of my first semester, I experienced a spiritual breakthrough that would define my life and ministry from that point on. It was an experience where I was immersed in God's love and power with extraordinary intensity. In that encounter, I had a tangible foretaste of the Kingdom life that Jesus made possible. And I haven't been the same since.[1]

I realize that this is not everyone's testimony. And I know that I'm not the only one who's ever confessed to spending more time learning about God than authentically experiencing his presence. Most believers hear and sing about God's goodness, power and freedom every weekend in their church gatherings. A number give sacrificially so that the "Good News" can be shared by missionaries somewhere far away. But if honest, many would confess that they are desperate for an authentic Kingdom encounter. Many have settled for less than what is promised and provided for according to the Word of God.

What contributes to this situation? A primary factor is that many believers have little appreciation for just how good the Good News of

---

[1] A detailed description of this experience is shared in chapter 3

the Kingdom really is. For these believers, Jesus' startling announcement that, "The Kingdom of God is at hand," provokes little response, let alone the revolution he intended. Jesus taught that when a person discovers the Kingdom they respond like someone who has found a pearl of great worth or a hidden treasure in a field. Such a person joyfully rearranges their whole life around that incomparable discovery (see Matthew 13:44-46). As a pastor, professor and now missionary, I've found that people most often lack fascination for God's Kingdom, along with having little desire to organize their lives around it, simply because they've never encountered it.

> *I've found that people most often lack fascination for God's Kingdom, along with having little desire to organize their lives around it, simply because they've never encountered it.*

The Good News is something much more than just having an assurance that you are going to be with Jesus when you die. It is more than just knowing and even believing things revealed in the Bible. The Good News is that Jesus is a conquering King and has made his Kingdom accessible to all who would exercise humility and courage to repent and receive it by faith. Those who enter the life Jesus made possible are ushered into a supernatural way of living under the reign and rule of God. To the faithful follower of Jesus, life is anything but ordinary as he or she experiences the things of heaven transforming the things of earth. Followers of this untamed King grow to expect the Spirit to show up and demonstrate the reality of God in tangible ways every day. In this Kingdom the guilty experience forgiveness, the wounded are healed, the bound are set free and the fearful are overwhelmed by God's transforming love. The King is making all things new.

Yet in a candid moment, many Christians would have to admit that though they are saved, they are far from set free and living such a life.

Others could confess that though they might be well informed, they have not been supernaturally transformed by the Good News of God. The good news of the Gospel is that Jesus has made the way for people to share an eternal, intimate and fruitful relationship with God. And this is not something only reserved for heaven. Jesus has made it possible for every believer to experientially know the love, truth and power of God in the here and now. From Christ's first coming to his return, we are meant to live expecting that we will experience tangible foretastes of God's Kingdom on earth as it is in heaven. To be sure, it's only a partial fulfillment until Jesus returns, but it's a reality for today and not a future hope alone. And this supernatural provision has been promised to all who seek to walk in an abiding relationship with God through Jesus Christ. This indeed is Good News!

For this reason, I was compelled to write this book. This message has been growing in me for decades. It is my life message. I have thoughtfully considered its themes through my years of academic reflection at Point Loma College (BA), Gordon-Conwell Theological Seminary (M.Div.) and Fuller Theological Seminary (D.Min.). Perhaps more importantly I have gained a fair amount of applied knowledge in the trench of Kingdom ministry as a church planter and pastor on both the East and West coasts of the United States; as a university and seminary professor; as a director of a spiritual formation retreat ministry; as a retreat facilitator and conference speaker on mission fields throughout the world; and as an equipper and coach to hundreds of emerging leaders through the years; as the founder of a training school for emerging leaders, and most recently as the Director of Pioneering Initiatives for ChurchNEXT, a ministry of Church Resource Ministries.

WHAT TO EXPECT FROM THIS BOOK

My hope is that those who read this book will grow to appreciate and experience the Kingdom life Jesus made possible. The following chapters will explain some of the most critical aspects of such a life. While each chapter can be read and understood independently, the first two chapters lay the foundational principles that make it possible to fully appreciate the rest of the book. Here is an overview of each chapter:

Chapter 1 - The Kingdom Within Our Reach

Jesus reveals that the gospel is the good news that his Kingdom is now accessible to all because he has come. The Kingdom can be defined as the effectual rule of God, which exists wherever God is having his way. The ministry of Jesus has opened the way for anyone who positively responds to his call to experience God's reigning presence in the here and now. Though Jesus has inaugurated the Kingdom of God at the time of his first coming, the Kingdom will not be consummated until his return. We currently live in the tension of the "now and not yet." This theological tension helps us understand, for example, why we sometimes pray for the sick and they are healed, and other times we pray and they are not. This chapter will explore the meaning of the Kingdom now among us, and emphasize the benefit of experiencing its tangible reality in our daily lives.

Chapter 2 – Disciples of the Risen King

At the core of the Great Commission is the command of Jesus for believers to make more and better disciples of Jesus who will serve to advance his Kingdom. This, along with knowing and loving God with all our heart, mind, soul and strength, is the central task of the spiritual life. A disciple is one who is learning to follow Jesus with the aim of becoming more like him in word and deed. While many seem to be looking for a quick and convenient way to grow spiritually, nothing short of Jesus' approach to formation can produce faithful and fruitful followers of Jesus. Leaders who want a discipleship program that neglects a tangible relationship with those they are "discipling" will contribute little to their formation or the advance of God's Kingdom. In this chapter, we will explore the critical components of an organic/relational approach to disciple formation, as well as the most common impediments to authentic spiritual growth.

Chapter 3 – Empowered by the Spirit

The example of Jesus and the early church as they advanced the Kingdom is unquestionably a concert of truth and power. As we read God's Word, we discover the necessity of God's power. As we encounter God's power, we discover that our desire for God's Word increases. Yet in the church today it seems many feel they must choose to emphasize either the truth of God's Word or the experiential power of the Spirit in their ministry settings. Disciples of the Risen King must embrace both as they seek to fulfill their mission to make more and better disciples of Jesus and advance his Kingdom. This failure to pursue a functional balance between truth and power explains the impoverished spiritual life and shallow Kingdom impact that is currently the reality for many Christians and ministries today. This chapter will highlight the importance of both truth and power. It will also cast a vision for why this balance is necessary for authentic disciple formation and missional impact. It is time for us to live and serve as empowered evangelicals!

Chapter 4 – Physical Healing Today

The God who never changes is still in the business of healing the sick and setting the captives free. The ministry of physical healing was and is a core component of the Good News of Jesus Christ. Yet few disciples today, especially in the Western context, have the same instinct of Jesus and the early Christians who offered to pray for the sick when confronted with the opportunity. In this chapter, we will consider the theological foundations for physical healing; the conditions conducive to divine healing; common questions regarding the ministry of healing; the relationship between the ministry of healing and discipleship; and how churches and individual believers can effectively minister to the sick.

Chapter 5 – Healing for the Broken Hearted

Though Jesus has placed his comfort, healing and inner freedom within the reach of anyone who would trust in him, many Christians today remain crippled by the failures and woundings of their past. The good news of Jesus Christ includes the healing of such pain. "It is for freedom that Christ has set us free" (Galatians 5:1); yet the unfinished business of our inner lives inevitably becomes a huge encumbrance to the freedom that Jesus has made possible. This chapter will examine how to overcome past woundings and failures, along with the connected ailments of resentment, depression, fear and the common lies under which many people live.

Chapter 6 – Welcome to the War!

It is doubtful that many believers hear the words, "Welcome to the war" soon after crossing the line of faith into relationship with Jesus. But perhaps they should in light of the reality of our strategic enemy. It is dangerously naïve for a Christ-follower to believe that they cannot be a target of the devil and his minions. Believers must learn how to recognize and effectively renounce demonic footholds in order to get free, stay free and set others free. This chapter will examine how a person can be set free from demonic entanglements and become equipped to do the same for others.

Chapter 7 – Making Space for God

The initial response to God's Kingdom invitation must be matched by a continuous cooperation with the demands of abiding under the rule of God. The call to the Kingdom is not first of all a call to power, a program, or even to Christian ministry. It is a call to love and follow Jesus Christ as his beloved friends. It's a call to live in a continuous, willing surrender to the reigning presence of God. The Bible reveals that a life oriented as such is not only possible but is the promised destiny to all who would commit themselves to it. But such a life will never happen without humility, serious intention and effort. This chapter will help the reader know how to embrace the spiritual practices that serve to enable a fruitful abiding life with Christ.

Chapter 8 – Making Space for Friends

A faithful and fruitful life in the Kingdom is made possible by a relational miracle between God and man. That miracle is meant to be experienced and supported in our relationships with others. We must each be encouraged and held accountable along the way, yet far too many believers today live isolated Christian lives. Perhaps the reason for this is that connecting with others is often marked with challenges, disappointments and pain. This chapter will consider what it takes to cultivate supportive friendships. And friends in such a community must be available and vulnerable to one another with Christ kept at the center.

WHY THIS BOOK IS IMPORTANT

This book is unique in that it offers an important balance between the theological meaning and the practical implications of the fact that Jesus made his reigning presence accessible to all who would repent and believe. Every chapter will offer a creative movement between explanation, illustration and application. Perhaps the information covered in each chapter is not so much "new" but rather has been made newly accessible to thoughtful evangelicals who truly thirst for the Spirit and hunger for the Word. On the other hand, it may be new to those who have not seen a practical, theologically satisfying book addressing themes such as the Kingdom of God, discipleship, spiritual formation, healing, the power of the Spirit, and the mission of the church. I believe that *The Life Jesus Made Possible* can serve as a strategic resource for any individual with a desire for personal spiritual formation in their lives; for those who need a comprehensive yet easy-to-understand book for those they are discipling; for pastors who desire to equip and release the saints for ministry, spiritual renewal, and missional activation; for students pursuing ministry training and wanting to complement their more theoretical education with applied theology; for small groups to use as an interactive curriculum; and for ministry training centers that are developing the next generation of those who will courageously follow Jesus and serve to advance his Kingdom.

May God bless you with his renewing and empowering presence as you read this book. Are you ready to explore and experience the Kingdom within your reach? Assuming you are, let's begin our journey to discover what it can mean to live the life Jesus made possible!

PART 1

THE MINISTRY JESUS MADE POSSIBLE

CHAPTER 1

THE KINGDOM WITHIN OUR REACH

After John was put in prison, Jesus went into Galilee, proclaiming the good news of God. "The time has come," he said. "The kingdom of God is near. Repent and believe the good news!"

Mark 1:14-15

The spiritual life is not a life then and there, but a life here and now. It is a life in which the Spirit of God is revealed in the ordinary encounters of everyday.[2]

Henri Nouwen

During my third year of college, I was trying to write a theology paper that just wasn't coming together in a way that made sense—even to me. I knew that true theology ought to satisfy both the mind and the heart, but my paper wasn't offering much to either. After researching and writing with ongoing frustration, I finally gave a call to my mentor and friend, Don Williams. He and I were colleagues at a local Presbyterian church where I was leading worship and heading up the youth ministry. Don had his PhD in New Testament, and I was hopeful that he could help me find a way forward.

That afternoon, Don and I got together to talk about my paper. He asked me to consider if there was one theme that could hold the whole paper together. After some thought and discussion, he introduced me to what I now see as the unifying theme of the Bible, that is, the Kingdom of God. As Don talked, I felt my paradigm shifting and a theological awakening happening that has since shaped my thinking over the last three decades. Now I see how the Kingdom

---

[2] From the cover of, Henri Nouwen, *Here and Now* (New York: Crossroad Publishing, 1997).

of God was meant to impact more than my theological sensibilities. It had everything to do with everything!

The Good News of the Kingdom

The meaning of the Greek word translated *gospel* is "good news." Jesus reveals that his news is good because his Kingdom has now been made accessible to all people through his coming as the God-Man to earth. His ministry opened the way for everyone to experience God's reigning presence in the here and now. The "good news" was not the introduction of the Kingdom, or the fact that one day the Kingdom would be consummated at the Second Coming of Christ. Jesus was not saying that the Kingdom was "about to come, or had recently come *into existence....* His Gospel concerned primarily the new accessibility of the Kingdom to humanity through himself."[3] And though the concept of the Kingdom was not new—and in fact, an understanding of God's Kingdom throughout history provides one of the clearest unifying factors in the Bible—what was new about Jesus' unprecedented message was that, through him, the Kingdom of God had now been placed within our reach! Derek Morphew writes:

> When we look at the Word of God from the perspective of the centrality of Christ, we realize that the message, ministry and self-understanding of Jesus are inseparably linked to the kingdom. Jesus came announcing the kingdom. His parables explained the kingdom, and his miracles bore witness to its presence. In fact, the theme of the kingdom as preached by Jesus Christ unites the whole flow of biblical truth, from Moses, through the Prophets, the Writings, the Gospels, the Epistles and the Revelation of John.[4]

---

[3] Dallas Willard, *The Divine Conspiracy* (San Francisco: Harper Collins, 1998), 26.
[4] Derek Morphew, *Breakthrough* (Cape Town, South Africa: Vineyard International Publishing, 1991), 8.

In Mark 1:14 we are told that, "After John was put in prison, Jesus went into Galilee, proclaiming the good news of God." Immediately following this, Mark quotes Jesus as he reveals the substance of that good news, saying, "The time has come. The Kingdom of God is near. Repent and believe the good news" (Mark 1:15). Let's examine the essence of this announcement.

The time has come. The first thing Jesus said as he proclaims the good news was a revolutionary disclosure for his Jewish audience. They had been waiting for many generations for their Messiah to come and bring a Kingdom breakthrough. Obviously, Jesus wouldn't have said this if *the time* had been in the past. Through Jesus, the epic event of all eternity had broken in upon humanity, and truly the world has never been the same.

In the Greek, which is the language of the New Testament, two words are used to describe "time." One is *chronos*, which is sequential time, and the other is *kairos*, which describes an opportune moment. *Chronos* time is what the nurse used when she reported that my first son had been born: "Andrew John Randall, born at 7:27 p.m. on January 6, 1985." But for me another kind of time had broken into that present moment. When I looked into the face of my baby boy, it was a *kairos* occurrence for me. It is these *kairos* moments invading *chronos* time that interrupt life as we know it. Time stood still as I watched my boy come into the world, and from that moment on, Jill's and my life would never be the same! Jesus' startling Good News announcement begins with just such a jolt: "The time has come, and from this moment on, life as you know it will never be the same." That is why this *kairos* event was indeed epic.

The Kingdom of God is near. The Kingdom of God—God's functional rule and reign—is what Jesus is now declaring that has broken into time. And Jesus revealed that this Kingdom is present wherever God is having his way in our lives or situations. The reign of God is not a place but "an event."[5] The Kingdom in Scripture "is not viewed spatially nor institutionally, but rather as the dynamic, active rule of God through Jesus Christ and the Holy Spirit."[6] Where there's sickness and the Kingdom comes, there's healing. When somebody's bound up demonically and the Kingdom is present, a person is set free. When a relationship is spinning out of control and the Kingdom moves in, there's reconciliation. When hope invades the heart of a person living on the edge of despair, the Kingdom is showing up.

Then Jesus tells us that the Kingdom is "near", which does not mean that the Kingdom is almost here. The Greek word translated in Mark 1:15 can be properly stated, *"at hand, drawing close, put within our reach."* So, the Good News that had broken into the world through the ministry of Jesus is that the Kingdom of God is now ours—literally within our reach!

What the Old Testament saints anticipated for centuries, Jesus ushered in with his first coming. With his *words*, Jesus proclaimed the message of the Kingdom, "The rule of God has come to earth and has been brought within your reach!" And with his *works* as he healed the sick, cast out demons, and raised the dead, he demonstrated the reality of his Kingdom message. It's important to note that the "good news" essentially includes both what Jesus declared and demonstrated with regard to his Kingdom now among us. It's both his *words* and *works*.

Today we live in the tension between the first and second comings of Jesus Christ. During this "age" we enjoy many of the benefits of the future age. God by his Spirit provides us with many foretastes of heaven, such as the experience of supernatural love, joy, peace and power, along with occasions of physical, emotional and spiritual healing. In heaven there will be no trace of deception, hatred, depression, anxiety, sickness, or bondage. There, the Enemy will not

---

[5] Morphew, 20.

[6] Charles Van Engen, *God's Missionary People* (Grand Rapids, Michigan: Baker Book House, 1991), 108, 109.

be present to "kill, steal and destroy" (John 10:10). And so, the Church often prays as Jesus taught, "Your Kingdom come and your will be done on earth as it is in heaven" (Matt. 6:10).

Yet, while Jesus truly inaugurated the Kingdom of God at his first coming, the Kingdom will not be consummated until his second and final return. This situation of "fulfillment without consummation"[7] translates into a certain eschatological tension for Christ followers, one that cannot be avoided in this present age without misrepresenting what Jesus reveals. We are *already* experiencing the reality of the Kingdom of God, but we are *not yet* experiencing it perfectly. Thus, the church lives "'between the times'; the old age goes on, but the powers of the new age have irrupted into the old age."[8] This mysterious reality means that until the second coming of Christ, we will experience healing *and* sickness. Pain *and* joy. Freedom *and* difficulty.

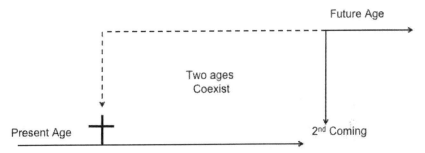

The existence of this tension helps us understand why there is such a struggle for believers to live consistently in the light of what God has made possible, and why the sick are often healed when prayed for, yet at other times they are not. The simple truth is that Christians live in a world that stands in opposition to God's right to rule. The dark powers of this world are both potent and strategic. Yet the barriers of this present darkness can be overcome through the grace that God has so richly provided. This occurs when the Gospel is applied to the spiritual and physical needs of our lives, when we are prepared for spiritual

7 Cf., George Eldon Ladd. *The Presence of the Future* (Grand Rapids: Eerdmans, 1974), 105ff.
8 Ladd, *Theology of the New Testament*. Revised Ed. (Grand Rapids: Eerdmans, 1993), 66,67.

battle, when we employ the spiritual disciplines, when we connect with other Christians who also obey and abide with God, and as we live in alignment with our God given calling and destiny.

It actually is possible to consistently remain under God's reign and rule in the very place we live our daily lives. Disciples of Jesus Christ can change and grow increasingly into the likeness of their Master because of the Father's love, the work of Christ, and the power of the manifest presence of God's Holy Spirit in their lives. Disciples of Jesus can continually abide in and advance the Kingdom of God, which is the good news that Jesus announced and ushered in.

Repent and believe the good news. Now that the Kingdom of God is at hand, we are called to embrace it through repentance and faith. Here Jesus was basically saying, "In light of what I've made available to you, it's time to create space for what you can now access freely by my grace. But in order to embrace my Kingdom, you must let go of some of the other things you're holding onto." And so, we say "no" to things that previously made sense before the Kingdom came within our reach. For Jesus' first disciples this would literally mean saying "no" to their occupations and even their families in order to say "yes" to following him. Many of us today may need to repent and say "no" to our attachments and those negative influences that cause us to live in fear and the need to try to maintain control of our circumstances. Doing so opens the way to sincerely believe and say "yes" to the benefits of humbly surrendering to the rule and reign of God every day.

Through repentance, we make room for a supernatural life under the reign and rule of God. And Jesus continues to make this invitation to us 2,000 years later. For though this amazing gift has been brought within our reach, abiding in the Kingdom is not automatic for Christ followers. The believer must choose to surrender and cooperate with God, to continually align his or her thinking and living to what God has made accessible. And by doing so, ordinary humans may experience the extraordinary life God has given us in his Kingdom.

MAKING SPACE FOR GOD'S KINGDOM

So, what is the motivation for and the outcome of choosing the life that Jesus made possible? Jesus says simply: "Repent for the Kingdom of heaven is near" (Matthew 4:17). In other words, *we repent in order to position ourselves to experience more and more of the life Jesus made possible.* There is nothing like a life being lived under the functional reign and rule of God, a life where God is fully having his way in every arena of our existence. Like Dave Ferguson of Community Christian Church describes, I like to call the person who is focused and moving in this direction a "3C Disciple." As I define it, this is a person who is **C**entered on Jesus, **C**onnected to supportive friends, and **C**ooperating in the mission of God.

Centered. Connected. Cooperating. A tangible commitment to these realities inevitably produces a fruitful life, one that is focused on God, one another, and what God is doing in the world today. I believe the testimony of Scripture reveals that a 3C lifestyle is what every follower of Jesus really *needs* in order to live the life He has made possible. That is why I often pray that God will make those in my relational orbit want what they really need, and what they really need will be what they sincerely want. Immediately after Jesus tells us to repent because the Kingdom that has been placed within our reach (Matthew 4:17), he begins calling people into a 3C Disciple lifestyle that will position them to experience all that is possible under his reign and rule.

Jesus calls us to Center our lives on Him

As Jesus was walking beside the Sea of Galilee, he saw two brothers, Simon called Peter and his brother Andrew. They were casting a net into the lake, for they were fishermen. "Come, follow me," Jesus said, "and I will make you fishers of men." At once they left their nets and followed him (Matthew 4:18-20).

To experience the life that Jesus made possible, we must center our lives on Him. And to have lives centered on Jesus, we need to cultivate a lifestyle of repentance—one of turning and returning to God again and again by living life under his reign and rule. We were created for a life where Jesus is at the center, where we do not merely visit his presence every once in a while, but where we constantly live in the awareness of his love, truth, presence, and power. This is called abiding with God (John 15:5), or "practicing his presence", as the famed monastic Brother Lawrence coined it. But for this to be a functional reality, we must create space in our daily routines where we can "turn to God" for the sake of gaining and maintaining spiritual focus and renewal. In these precious times of solitude and focus, we converse with God in prayer as we reflect on Scripture in his presence. But we must also learn to carry the richness of our solitude into the predictable rhythms, as well as the unexpected interruptions, of our daily life. More about how to do this in Chapter 7.

Jesus calls us to Connect with supportive friends

> *Going on from there, he saw two other brothers, James son of Zebedee and his brother John. They were in a boat with their father Zebedee, preparing their nets. Jesus called them, and immediately they left the boat and their father and followed him* (Matthew 4:21,22).

One thing is certain: to be a disciple who fruitfully abides with Jesus, we must commit to doing so with others who are committed to doing the same. If asked, most believers say they desire to center their lives on Jesus as a sustained reality. But because of our weaknesses and the many distractions in life, this is far from a simple matter. To remain centered on Jesus we need others to encourage us and hold us accountable in practical and consistent ways. And for this to happen, there needs to be people in our lives with whom we are tangibly available and vulnerable on a regular basis. The Lord never called us to make this journey alone. He put us in a body for a reason, and that is essential if we are going to access all that Jesus made possible.

The writer to the Hebrews stresses this point clearly; "And let us consider how we may spur one another on toward love and good deeds, not giving up meeting together, as some are in the habit of doing, but encouraging one another…." (Hebrews 10:24,25). Every disciple of Jesus needs friends with whom he or she can truly live the life Jesus made possible. That is why Jesus calls us to repent, to turn away from our independent instincts and intentionally make room in our busy schedules to authentically and unhurriedly connect with supportive friends who are seeking to follow Jesus as well. We must connect with others in order to encourage one another (put courage in) to keep believing God, even when it is hard. We must keep showing up even when it would be easier to quit or go it alone, to keep deciding to obey God even after feeling ashamed because others have seen our failures. Chapter 8 is dedicated to the critical subject of connecting in an authentic Christian community.

Jesus calls us to Cooperate in the mission of God

Jesus went throughout Galilee, teaching in their synagogues, preaching the good news of the kingdom, and healing every disease and sickness among the people (Matthew 4:23).

Not only does Jesus invite us to follow him—and do so with others who are also walking with him—he also invites us to join him in what he is saying and doing in the world today. Like Jesus' first followers, the Lord has invited us to repent and reposition our lives so we are in the middle of what he is doing. As I once heard Dallas Willard say, "A disciple is one who is learning to say and do what Jesus would if he were in our place." The journey of following the Lord with others includes the adventure of participating in the mission of God together. The moment we were forgiven of our sins and made spiritually alive by his Holy Spirit, we became members of his Body on earth, and simultaneously commissioned to say and do what Jesus desires to be said and done in the world in which we live. And until the believer both appreciates and embraces this truth, he or she will not be fully experiencing the life that Jesus made possible.

We certainly are not all shaped the same way for the same role in God's mission field, but every true believer has been uniquely made *on purpose for a purpose*[9] that contributes to the advancement of God's Kingdom. The sad fact is that if we don't repent and turn to Jesus so that our God-shaped need for adventure can be filled by cooperating in his mission, we will seek adventure elsewhere. This heart-felt void will not go unattended! When someone does not feel alive on the inside, engaging in crazy and even dangerous antics can begin to make sense. Rather than embracing some risky unrighteous adventure to fill the void, Jesus invites us to join him in his epic campaign to announce and demonstrate that his Kingdom has been placed within our reach. Nothing is more exciting than seeing a friend you love enter into a relationship with Jesus or receive divine healing or freedom from demonic strongholds.

This is the life that Jesus made possible, a life that is centered on him, one that is connected to supportive friends, and one where cooperating in his mission is a given. It is a fruitful and fulfilling life lived under the functional rule of God.

OTHER GOSPELS

Unfortunately, the good news of God has been challenged since the time of Jesus by "other gospels" that serve to distort what God provides. The apostle Paul speaks of this reality when writing the church at Galatia and refers to "a different gospel – which is really no gospel at all" (Galatians 1:6,7). I believe there are at least three examples of "other gospels" which currently have a wide influence in

---

[9] I believe this phrase was first coined by Rick Warren.

the body of Christ and must be interpreted as demonic gospel distortions:

The gospel of Jesus plus – The apostle Paul wrote that if anyone attempts to add anything to the gospel of grace, including any kind of religious works or rigor that must be exercised to earn a right relationship with God, then you are no longer talking about the true gospel. We can never be made right with God via correct behavior or belief, even on our best day.

Paul was exceptionally angry with those who perverted the good news in this way. Unfortunately, the "gospel of *Jesus plus*" is still proclaimed by many in today's world. It's most basic manifestation is works-righteousness or legalism, which finds its way in some form into almost every corner of the body of Christ. This perversion of the gospel is not only damaging, it is contagious. Perhaps this is why Paul, as well as Jesus, confronted legalism with such forcefulness. For example, the Judaizing teachers in Galatia seduced the Gentile believers with the lie that they needed more than just a relationship with Jesus in order to be in right standing with God. They also needed to keep the Mosaic Law. In response to this, Paul wrote:

> Evidently some people are throwing you into confusion and are trying to pervert the gospel of Christ. But even if we or an angel from heaven should preach a gospel other than the one we preached to you, let him be eternally condemned! (Galatians 1:7,8).

Paul took this issue of legalism very seriously! As a recovering performance-driven people-pleaser, I must keep a close eye on my own heart regarding the "gospel plus." In fact, I believe the entire body of Christ must remain vigilant about the subtle and not so subtle ways this aberration creeps into the church, since it is in dangerous opposition to the gracious good news of Jesus Christ. When someone discovers themselves under the influence of a performance-oriented distortion of the gospel, they must quickly turn back to the God of grace and linger long in the truth of his abundant love and mercy. To the Galatians, who had at least temporarily succumbed to the gospel of *Jesus plus*, the apostle Paul writes these encouraging words; "It is for freedom that Christ has set us free. Stand firm, then, and do not let yourselves be burdened again by a yoke of slavery" (Galatians 5:1).

The gospel of sin management – Another popular distortion that many believers are attracted to is what Dallas Willard describes as "the gospel of sin management".[10] In this scenario, a person celebrates the fact that they have been forgiven more than they celebrate being set free from the domination of sin. Under this gospel's influence, more focus is given to organizing, covering up and compensating for sin than to simply renounce and overcome it. Concerning the popular bumper sticker that reads, "Christians Aren't Perfect, Just Forgiven," Willard writes:

> Just forgiven? And is that really all there is to being a Christian? The gift of eternal life comes down to that? Quite a retreat from living an eternal kind of life now! …Christians certainly aren't perfect. There will always be need for improvement. But there is a lot of room between being perfect and being "just forgiven" as that is nowadays understood. You could be much more than forgiven and still not be perfect. Perhaps you could even be a person in whom Jesus' eternal kind of life predominates and still have room for growth."[11]

One of the most glorious truths of the good news of the Kingdom is that sinful people can be graciously and completely forgiven, but the good news doesn't stop there. It is even "gooder" than that! The redemptive work of Christ and the provision of his Spirit open the way for full forgiveness as well as liberating freedom from sin's control.

---

[10] Dallas Willard, *The Divine Conspiracy*, Chapter 2.
[11] Willard, 35,36

> No temptation has seized you except what is common to man. And God is faithful; he will not let you be tempted beyond what you can bear. But when you are tempted, he will also provide a way out so that you can stand up under it (1 Corinthians 10:13).

Yes, we are not called to simply manage, endure or cover up our sin; we have been invited to overcome it through surrender to Jesus Christ in the power of the Holy Spirit.

The gospel of then and there – This alteration of the gospel removes much of its efficacy from the present to times past or in the future. Thanks to dispensational or cessational theology, many evangelicals are bound to a truncated view of the gospel where much of the supernatural workings of the Spirit recorded in Scripture are deemed no longer available or necessary (now that the biblical canon is complete). Rather than embracing the gospel of the Kingdom as a relevant *here and now* reality, it is presented as a temporary provision for the *then and there*, or the *someday and somewhere*. John Calvin, a prominent theologian of the reformation, puts forth this view when he writes:

> The gift of healing, like the rest of the miracles, which the Lord willed to be brought forth for a time, has vanished away in order to make the preaching of the gospel marvelous forever...Healing now has nothing to do with us, to whom the administering of such powers has not been committed.[12]

Such a dramatic departure from a straightforward interpretation of Scripture is an indication of a reactionary mindset. What likely motivated Calvin to dissociate from miracles was his desire to undercut the Roman Catholic claim to religious authority based on miracles and extra-biblical revelation. Upon examination, however, one finds that most Christian teachings that dismiss the miraculous from current

---

[12] John Calvin, *Institutes*, 1467

times find their origin in a reactionary context rather than an honest, exegetical reflection. Making this point, Derek Morphew writes:

> Cessationism probably arose as an explanation for the dearth of signs and wonders in the drier periods of church history, aided by fanatics who brought signs and wonders into disrepute during and after the Reformation. This caused more sober Reformed leaders to react in the opposite direction: knowledge of the Word and faith in Jesus Christ was said to be all a Christian must desire. Added to this was an emphasis on the dangers of "subjectivism". People were told to be careful about becoming too subjective about their faith as this could lead to all sorts of fanaticism: we must base our faith on the Word, which is objective, not on subjective experiences.[13]

And perhaps no one has made the case for the cessation of the miraculous with more impact in this past century than B.B. Warfield in his book, *Counterfeit Miracles*, published in 1918. To this day, this book is still regarded by many as a theological masterpiece, though careful exegetical evidence is sorely lacking throughout. Warfield insisted that miracles were a temporary provision given strictly to accredit biblical doctrine. Once the Bible became a credible authority, miracles were no longer needed. What this view fails to appreciate is that supernatural signs are indications of God's supremacy and his abiding presence among us. Wonders, signs, and miracles are provided today to point people to God and advance his Kingdom on earth just like they did when Jesus was here 2,000 years ago.

Warfield believed in a "wonder-working God, but not in a wonder-working church."[14] But where is the biblical evidence for that? To the Corinthians, Paul wrote that a demonstration of the Spirit's power

---

[13] Morphew, 171
[14] Warfield, *Counterfeit Miracles*, 58.

accompanied his preaching, "so that your faith might not rest on men's wisdom, but on God's power" (1 Cor. 2:5). He later writes that the very nature of the Kingdom among us will include demonstrations of God's power (1 Cor. 4:20). The writer to the Hebrews reveals that God himself testifies to our salvation "by signs, wonders, and various miracles, and gifts of the Holy Spirit distributed according to his will" (Hebrews 2:4). Nowhere does the Bible itself reveal that God no longer intends for a wonder-working church. In fact, the very opposite is true.

Because we have been called to say and do what Jesus' first followers said and did, we desperately need what they were promised and lived in light of. How can we truly represent Jesus with less? The enemy we overcome through announcing God's Kingdom is no cessationist, though surely he must delight when the church embraces such doctrinal fallacy. It is good news that we can humbly follow and obey the One who is the same today, yesterday and forever, and we are privileged to live and serve under the same promise of the Spirit's power given to those who journeyed before us. It is clear from Scripture that the only gospel Jesus proclaimed was the gospel of the Kingdom, and he has commissioned us to live and proclaim the same Kingdom until he comes again! "And this gospel of the Kingdom will be preached in the whole world as a testimony to all nations, and then the end will come" (Matthew 24:14).

> *When there is a great chasm between our doctrine and our practice, it is what we do that will expose what we really believe.*

It's amazing that such reactionary thinking has been repeated by so many through the last century. But at least cessationists and dispensationalists are consistent and honest about what they believe and practice. I am more concerned about the common discrepancies that exist among those who profess to believe in God's power to heal today, yet seldom (if ever) pray with the expectation that God will show up and actually heal the person. When there is a great chasm between our doctrine and our practice, it is what we do that will expose what we really believe. Many would never admit that they were a theological dispensationalist or cessationist, even though, for the sake of honesty, the term "functional cessationist" could be used to describe them. Regarding the miraculous, I have a personal passion to see every leader and believer reclaim not only a doctrine of miracles but also the Christ-like instinct to immediately respond to sickness and bondage with expectant prayer.

THE NEED FOR A LEADERSHIP REVOLUTION

For the whole church to embrace the Kingdom that Jesus placed within our reach, its leaders must passionately teach and minister in Kingdom truth and power. Yet with consideration to how most leaders are equipped, is it any wonder that very little supernatural activity goes on in the segment of the body of Christ they lead? I believe there is a critical need for us to honestly assess the manner in which our leaders are being shaped for ministry by our theological institutions. The countless Scriptures that deal with such things as healing, deliverance, and hearing God's voice are seldom studied for practical application. And few, if any, courses are offered that equip leaders to function with skill in these areas. A disciple who is formed in a learning environment where the priority of exegetical and theological reflection leaves little or no room for experience and practical application can only multiply followers who believe and behave in kind.

In his book, *Breaking Tradition To Accomplish Vision*, Sherwood Lingenfelter writes:

> The weakness of formal education is the absence of experience within which to process the data. The formal method provides information without context and with very little practice, so the student does not see its relationship to life...Information without character

or skill development can lead to a very frustrating and dangerous end.[15]

It should not surprise us that most of the institutionally trained leaders who enter vocational ministry today are forced (or choose) to find something else to do within a few years. Learning from lectures, books, and research certainly has its place, but it is not enough. Without intentional spiritual and character formation, along with "in the trench" training in practical ministry, what sort of disciples and leaders are we shaping? Bottom line, for what are the traditional ministry training institutions preparing its disciples and future leaders? Sadly, surveys show that the "overwhelming majority of [seminary graduates] feel unprepared for the ministry challenges they face as they enter the service of churches."[16]

Perhaps a serious look at the approach Jesus used to train the first generation of Kingdom servants is now in order for many schools. Jesus frowned upon the fact that people can know a lot *about* God and the Bible and never really *know* God himself or his power for ministry. To the most religiously trained Jewish leaders, Jesus said, "You are in error because you do not know the Scriptures or the power of God" (Matthew 22:29). Commenting on this, Rich Nathan writes:

> The religious leaders of Israel were doing what comes naturally to human beings: missing the forest for the trees. They had come to view the study of the Holy Scriptures as an end in itself, rather than as the inspired means to the end of a personal encounter with the living God. They reduced religion to a set of precepts and principles, but in the process missed the person.[17]

---

15 Gupta, Paul and Lingenfelter, Sherwood. *Breaking Tradition To Accomplish Vision.* (BMH Books, 2006), 51.
16 McNeal, *Revolution In Leadership,* 119.
17 Nathan, Rich; Wilson, Ken (2009-07-07). Empowered Evangelicals (Kindle Locations 1633-1637). Ampelon Publishing. Kindle Edition.

How unfortunate that since the time of Jesus people can be satisfied with *"belief-about-God* rather than *belief-in-God* himself."[18] How sad that so many Christian leaders have only been taught to manage the Bible and grow the church, rather than truly equip the saints for authentic Kingdom impact. I wonder what course requirements and learning outcomes Jesus would put into his syllabus if he were teaching a seminary course today?

Regarding the contrast between what Jesus called us to, as compared to our current reality, Rich Nathan says:

> Unfortunately, pastors may not be expected to be able to cast out demons, heal the sick, or even evangelize the lost; but in the effectively-led large church, pastors will be expected to draft a meaningful mission statement for the church, articulate the church's values and vision, delegate authority, preside over boards and committees, set reasonable goals and timetables for achieving those goals, manage budgets, and write job descriptions. Are our standards of measuring large church pastors really derived from the Bible? Even our training of seminarians tends to place a premium on human technique and control.[19]

A seminary student recently shared with me that during an entire course on the subject of healing, the class never actually prayed for the sick or even talked about how to do that. The professor, who professed to believe that God heals today, did not equip the students or encourage them to launch healing ministries in their churches back home. Unfortunately, many God-loving, Bible-believing leaders have unintentionally been equipped to preach and teach a truncated gospel that may inform their people but falls short of seeing the Kingdom

---

[18] Alan Hirsch, *Untamed: reactivating a missional form of discipleship.* (Grand Rapids: Baker Books, 2010), 91.
[19] Nathan, Kindle Locations 1091-1096

come on earth as it is in heaven. Regarding this situation Derek Morphew writes;

> In the Western world people are accustomed to concepts rather than practice. To the Hebrew mind, thinking, doing and being are part of one indivisible whole. Words are deeds and teachings are practices. Jesus taught within the framework of rabbinical techniques of discipleship.[20]

This is where most theological institutions are stuck and, therefore, not effectively producing disciples that do what Jesus did. And this is why I am so encouraged by a fresh movement of missional outposts around the world that are reclaiming their primary responsibility for equipping emerging leaders for effective service in the Kingdom—as pastors, church planters, and missionaries serving in every crevice of culture. Because the church forgets how to do what it has outsourced, it will not be a quick or painless transition to church-based, in the trench equipping, but it must happen.

I honestly believe we will always need specialized institutions for training. As someone with an earned doctorate, I have much to be grateful for with regard to my education through the traditional track. It has opened doors for me that I believe have been strategic in the fulfillment of my destiny. But the fields are far too ripe to limit ministry to those who have been legitimatized as vocational servants only by accredited institutions.

In my opinion, every church committed to the advance of the Kingdom needs to find creative, innovate ways to reclaim leadership development in their local settings. Perhaps a group of like-minded churches in the same region could collaborate to provide a strategic training system for their emerging leaders. Over the past three decades my wife and I have sacrificially poured into hundreds of emerging

---

[20] Morphew, 134

leaders and have launched and led several ministries designed to address this need. Today we serve as full time missionaries with Church Resource Ministries, which has freed us to give our full attention to equipping and coaching emerging and existing leaders and teams worldwide. In fact, it is the primary focus in my new role as the Director of Pioneering Initiatives to discover, develop and deploy a new crop of courageous, apostolic leaders and teams committed to making disciples and launching new communities of faith from among the harvest worldwide. Such revolutionaries often find it difficult to function well in the main flow of institutional Christianity and are often the first to be marginalized by the status quo.

Regarding the equipping of such leaders, I have found that my heart resonates with a similar vision expressed over 100 years ago by A.B. Simpson, the founder of the Christian and Missionary Alliance, who explained his rationale for launching The Missionary Training Institute (now Nyack College) in New York, by saying:

> We do not compete in this institute with the regular theological seminary and the ordinary methods of taking the gospel ministry. We claim to be raising up a band of irregular soldiers for the vast unoccupied fields to supplement the armies of the Lord in the regions they cannot reach and work they cannot overtake.[21]

CONCLUSION

However it is pursued, the Church must find a way to functionally make more and better disciples of Jesus who prioritize his central message and ministry. Every member of the body of Christ must find their unique way to take all that God has given them and give it all away to others who will do the same with others who will do the same

---

[21] http://www.nyack.edu/about/nyack-history/MTI1933_01.

with others. We must seek first God's Kingdom (Matthew 6:33) and live and proclaim the life that Jesus has put within our reach!

CHAPTER 2

DISCIPLES OF THE RISEN KING

So far as the visible Christian institutions of our day are concerned, discipleship is clearly optional.

- Dallas Willard

Follow me.

- Jesus

I will never forget the first time I experienced the intense feeling that God really loved me, desired to forgive me of all my sins and be the center of my life. When I crossed the line of faith as a sophomore in high school, little did I know the extent of what this reality would provide. The experience left me both excited and curious as to where this might all lead. The youth leaders immediately gave me a Bible and taught me the basics of spending time with Jesus every day.

I also remember learning how to share my faith with others. I became an excited young follower of Jesus and shared about him with anyone who would listen. I was not ashamed of being a believer, advertising my faith on T-shirts and the bumper of my 63 Volkswagen Beetle. In the years to follow I had the privilege of introducing numerous family members and friends to Jesus. We often packed into my car and drove down to the San Diego Calvary Chapel to hear the young Mike McIntosh preach, along with amazing music from the likes of Chuck Girard, Parable and the Sweet Comfort Band. I was experiencing God's supernatural favor in those years when the Jesus Movement was exploding.

One day Mike called me over to talk about my new-found relationship with the Lord. He was a local Christian bookstore owner who looked and sounded like a totally legit hippie. Soon I would discover that Mike was a very profound, well-read thinker, and communicator of the gospel. After sharing some of my story with him, including the fact that I had just been elected student body president of my high school, Mike asked, "Hey man, how are you going to use this new position for Jesus?" I wasn't sure what he meant, but he clarified, "You don't think Jesus gave you this promotion without a reason, do you?"

Mike's question started a discussion that generated a crazy vision of launching a Christian club at my high school. Though many people told me that such a thing was illegal and could never happen, by the second month of my senior year the "Maranatha Club" was meeting weekly as a recognized entity at Escondido High School. Beyond studying the Bible and praying for each other at our weekly gatherings, we sponsored several retreats and hosted a number of concerts on campus. Before the year ended dozens of my friends had given their lives to Christ.

I continued meeting with Mike through my senior year. We would hang out at the store as well as at his house where I became part of his family. I even traveled with Mike when he spoke and ministered in various settings. Early on Mike didn't say much to me about spiritual gifts and being anointed for ministry, but occasionally it would leak out. Mike was careful because he could tell that I was more than a little cautious about all things "charismatic." The church I attended held an openly dispensational position regarding spiritual gifts and the work of the Spirit, which was overtly passed on to new believers. So, when Mike eventually brought up spiritual gifts and the power of the Spirit, I attempted to change the subject. I'm so grateful for Mike and the patient, loving and wise way he led me from being closed to the Holy Spirit, to open and interested. He did this largely through his life testimony that radiated a radical love for Jesus. Though at that time I didn't have a supernatural encounter with the Holy Spirit, my theological leaning was opened to the truth that Jesus is the same today, yesterday and forever, and that his provision of spiritual power for Kingdom life had never been revoked.

After graduating I headed off to prepare for ministry at Point Loma College. While I appreciated what I learned in that academic environment, it didn't compare to what Mike and my ministry experiences had taught me. Though I was unaware of it, Mike was intentionally discipling me to become a faithful and fruitful follower of the Risen King. Every believer needs a Mike!

WHAT IS A DISCIPLE?

Though the term "disciple" is used more than 200 times in the gospels and 28 times in the book of Acts, the significance of this word is not fully appreciated today by many in the body of Christ. Recently during a small group gathering, the guys headed out to the back porch while the gals remained in the living room for a time of sharing and prayer. As occasionally happens, we had a guest that night who was not yet a follower of Jesus. Steve asked if he could get some clarification on what he experienced that night. We all said "sure," unaware of where the discussion was going. As he began to process his thoughts Steve eventually asked, "What is a disciple?" As the group attempted to answer, I discovered that Steve was not the only one who wasn't clear on what a disciple is and what discipleship entails. These guys who had been believers for years had a difficult time articulating their thoughts about this fundamental reality of the Christian faith.

At its core, a disciple is a learner, student, or apprentice of someone. In the New Testament gospels, the word "disciple" predominately describes someone who is a follower of Jesus. It can also simply designate a believer in Jesus. In the early church, there was no concept of being a believer and not being a disciple. They were one and the same. Unfortunately, some hold to a mistaken view that the terms "believer" and "disciple" describe two different levels of commitment in a Christian's life. With this mindset, such a person might be a believer for some time before they are ready to commit to be a disciple. But the notion that a person could believe in Jesus without following and obeying him contradicts the very nature of true faith (see James 2:14). The evidence that you believe in Jesus is seen when you trust him with your life, intending to learn, grow, and become increasingly like him.

The believer's commitment to learn to obey *everything* Jesus commands is critical to discipleship. This is the epicenter of Jesus' Great Commission, "All authority in heaven and on earth has been given to me. Therefore go and make disciples of all nations, baptizing them in the name of the Father and of the Son and of the Holy Spirit, *and teaching them to obey everything I have commanded you.* And surely I am with you always, to the very end of the age" (Matthew 28:18-20, emphasis added). Overlooking the command to be obedient is what Dallas Willard calls the "great omission of the Great Commission."[22] Or as Dietrich Bonhoeffer put it, "Christianity without discipleship is always Christianity without Christ."[23]

While the expectation can never be *perfection* in our obedience to everything Jesus commanded, our lives can certainly demonstrate a measurable *progression* in that direction. This was the apostle Paul's attitude when he described his own journey of growth and formation.

> Not that I have already obtained all this, or have already been made perfect, but I press on to take hold of that for which Christ Jesus took hold of me. Brothers, I do not consider myself yet to have taken hold of it. But one thing I do: Forgetting what is behind and straining toward what is ahead, I press on toward the goal to win the prize for which God has called me heavenward in Christ Jesus (Phillipians 3:12-14).

---

[22] Dallas Willard, *The Great Omission: Reclaiming Jesus' Essential Teachings on Discipleship.* HarperCollins, 2006.

[23] Dietrich Bonhoeffer, *The Cost of Discipleship* (New York: Macmillan, 1937), 64.

A few key questions that can serve to reveal the reality of our discipleship include: 1) Am I focused on and moving toward Jesus and the life he made possible? 2) Am I becoming in actual practice more like Jesus day by day?

The fact that people continue to disobey and live in misalignment to the revealed will of God exposes that their life is unsurrendered in that area. And "teaching them to obey" implies that there must be an intentional process to bring Jesus' disciple to the point where his or her automatic responses are becoming increasingly like those of Jesus if he were in their place.

> *The ability to obey everything Jesus commanded is not something you can pull off without preparation, but rather is something learned in the context of discipleship.*

I can't count the times a seemingly "good" Christian man or woman has told me, "I don't know how this affair happened to me!" Or, "I don't know how I got into this situation!" In such cases the person did not have a tangible plan in place when tempted that was designed to help them remain focused and moving toward Jesus in the face of a challenging temptation. The lack of such a plan predictably set up the conditions where moral failure became their automatic response. The ability to obey everything Jesus commanded is not something you can pull off without preparation, but rather is something learned in the context of discipleship.

WHAT IS DISCIPLESHIP?

The term *disciple* refers to someone committed to following and obeying Jesus and becoming more like him. The term *discipleship* describes the intentional plan the disciple engages to realize that goal. But there are two common obstacles that the disciple must confront if authentic transformation is to take place: 1) programmatic thinking and 2) legalism.

The problem of programmatic thinking

Being made in the image of God who exists as a perfect, loving Triune community, we are inherently relational creatures. Hence, authentic discipleship is more an organic, relational process than a program. It is "being with Jesus learning to be like Him" as a holistic way of life, as I once heard Dallas Willard summarize it. Rather than a checklist of certain beliefs and behaviors, discipleship is a deliberate lifestyle of gaining focus and movement toward Jesus and the life He made possible. While this doesn't happen without an intentional plan, it is imperative to keep the end in mind, which is tangibly becoming more like Jesus in word and deed. Far too many people have worked through a discipleship curriculum without becoming more willing and courageous to obey the teachings of God's Word and the leading of his Spirit than they were when they began. Discipleship is more than classes, conferences and 3-ring binders. Putting into practice what one is learning in real life with tangible encouragement and accountability by others is imperative if Jesus-like transformation is to be attained.

Through the years I have often been asked to provide the "curriculum" we use to develop and deploy emerging leaders into active Kingdom service. They are often disappointed when I share that we primarily spend lots of intentional time with the young adults. We host gatherings in our living room, drink coffee together in town, do ministry together and then debrief, all the while employing large doses of patience! Sure, we offered numerous themes for discussion from the Bible and other leadership books and personality profiles. But a relational connection is measured in quality and quantity of time spent in dialogue and prayer. Without this ingredient, I doubt little of lasting value would have taken place.

The problem of legalism

Legalism is one of the greatest enemies of authentic discipleship. Countless times I've heard people tell me that they love Jesus but can't stand Christians or the church, at least as they have experienced them.

But what they often can't stand is actually the grotesque distortion of the gospel of grace and the life Jesus has truly made possible. The impact of legalism leads you either to live as a bound-up rule keeper or a reactionary rebel, and both display the ugly face of religious legalism.

At a recent spiritual formation retreat I asked the participants to describe the behaviors of a "good Christian" (with a little sarcasm in my tone so they would know what I was looking for). They offered a long list of things that such a person would do, such as go to church whenever the doors were open, read their bible daily, pray a lot, tithe, believe all the right doctrines and share their faith with others. They also listed numerous things a good Christian would NOT do. Not surprisingly, smoking, drinking, listening to worldly music, and hanging out with the wrong friends topped the list. Then I asked the participants to describe some of the common attitudes they've observed in these so-called "good Christians." They shot back words like proud, judgmental, angry, depressed, lonely, ashamed and weary. We eventually concluded that such a religious system leads one to exhaustion, hypocrisy or rebellion. Unfortunately, while many do rebel against the legalistic paradigm of discipleship, that objection itself doesn't lead to freedom but rather to a continued focus on the very religious system they are now opposing.

Bounded-Set Spirituality

Anthropologist Paul Hiebert describes this legalistic distortion as a symptom of a "bounded-set" approach to Christian formation.[24] The "bounded-set" can be described as a social system "that has clearly delineated boundaries but no strong ideological center."[25] The attractive benefit of the bounded-set paradigm is that you can know precisely if you or someone else is "in" or "out" based on specific beliefs and behaviors. You can seemingly gain and maintain control of

---

[24] Hiebert, Paul G. 1978. 'Conversion, Culture and Cognitive Categories'. *Gospel in Context* 1 (4):24-29.
[25] Hirsch, *Untamed*, 152.

your standing with God, and at the same time serve as a referee on God's behalf with regard to how others stand. It is a form of "checklist Christianity" at its worst. This approach to the Christian life predictively leads to strife, pride (and/or shame based on your performance) and an unending litany of judgment and condemnation of one's self and others. Bounded-set religion as described above is one of the most destructive symptoms of legalism. Criticizing this form of religion, the apostle Paul writes;

> Such regulations indeed have an appearance of wisdom with the self-imposed worship, their false humility and their harsh treatment of the body, but they lack any value in restraining sensual indulgence" (Colossians 2:23).

Just prior to this indictment, Paul describes the dysfunctional and fruitless religious system that believers need to reject if they hope to gain true spiritual maturity and freedom. This system includes the powerless rituals of religion (vv. 16,17), the revelations of the super-spiritual (vv. 18,19), and the vigor of asceticism (vv. 20-23). Then in chapter 3 Paul directs his readers to refocus their attention on the Person of Christ and the life he has made possible. In versus 1-4 Paul exhorts believers to set their hearts and minds on things above. Specifically, the believer is encouraged to focus on their *past* victory won by Christ, their *present* identity in Christ, and their *promised* hope guaranteed with Christ. Then in verses 5ff., Paul exhorts the Colossian community to work together to become in actual practice what they already are as the beloved of God through the work of Christ. Paul's ancient correction still needs to be received in many Christian circles today.

Centered-Set Formation

The bottom line is that the bounded-set approach to living the life that Jesus made possible is destined to fail. Jesus never called us to "keep the rules," but rather he declared, "Follow me!" The difference is that of *hollow rule keeping* versus *life-giving relationship* that is centered on Jesus under the influence of the Holy Spirit. Hiebert describes this New Testament paradigm for Christian formation as "centered-set" as opposed to "bounded-set."

The centered-set approach to formation celebrates focus and movement on the way to becoming more like Jesus rather than concentrating on right beliefs and behaviors in order to belong. And rather than comparing and competing, supportive friends who embrace a centered-set spirituality learn to encourage and hold one another accountable to their mutual commitment to being faithful followers of the Risen King. And when we shift our formation paradigm to emphasize focus and movement toward Jesus as the goal, a church leader's role shifts from being a control freak to becoming a revealer and encourager. Alan and Debra Hirsch describe this renovation of perspective in their book called, *Untamed: reactivating a missional form of discipleship*. In it they write:

> In the beginning of our ministry, we mistakenly saw it as our role to take control of their lives – to make right choices on their behalf - hoping that it would turn their lives around. In almost every case this failed. Deliverance came to us when it dawned on us that it was not our role to control people, but rather to bring

them into an authentic relationship with God. He would do all the changing that was needed.[26]

The wide acceptance of the bounded-set paradigm exposes the fact that many really don't believe that God will do all the changing that is necessary if we simply do our part to faithfully reveal Jesus and encourage people on their journey toward him. With the salvation of the lost and the true sanctification of the saved at stake, it is past time for the church to draw the line on this insidious enemy to authentic discipleship.

Being the friend of sinners

A few years ago, a student of mine from Simpson University wrote me a note that revealed the anguish that she experienced when stepping beyond the bounded-set idea of holiness in order to connect with pre-Christian friends. Earlier that week I had emphasized the courage required to follow Jesus across the street as opposed to just remaining safe in our Christian ghettos. I also shared about my own missed opportunities in the past to connect with my drinking neighbors for fear of being judged by other believers who lived in that same neighborhood. Here's the email:

> Dr. Randall,
>
> I am getting judged because of who my friends are and what they do in their life. I get judged because I hang out with them. My so-called Christian friends look down upon me, or question my belief because I will go to a bar with my friends. It was really encouraging on Saturday when you (Bill) were talking about how you regret not going to your neighbor's house and hanging out with them, even though they were drinking a few too many beers. The funny thing is that Jesus would likely have joined those garage conversations with his neighbors. I had this new sense of

---

[26] Alan Hirsch & Debra Hirsch, *Untamed: reactivating a missional form of discipleship.* (Baker Books, 2010), 156,157.

love over the weekend for Jesus. He thought outside of the box, and that's how I want to think. I don't like to live in this bubble that Christians put around us. Jesus would go where no one would even dream about going. How do we reach the poor, the hurt, and the lost if we can't even go to our neighbor's house?

That last question is the clincher. It underscores yet another reason why every true disciple of Jesus needs to be liberated from the bounded-set paradigm. How can I follow Jesus and become the "friend of sinners" if I can't even cross my street because I am hampered by the fear of being judged by believers for being worldly? Religion sucks! Western Christians do not need another training event or more resources to reach the lost. We simply need a courage awakening that can set us free to radically follow Jesus who leads his Church *into* the world while not being *of* it (cf., John 17:15-19).

THE ABIDING LIFE OF A FRUITFUL DISCIPLE

Though authentic discipleship is organic and relational, it still must be very intentional. John 15:5 offers Jesus' foundational promise to his followers concerning the spiritual dynamics that contributes to a fruitful life. In this text Jesus declares; *"I am the vine; you are the branches. If a man remains in me and I in him, he will bear much fruit; apart from me you can do nothing."* Among other things a disciple of Jesus is one dedicated to an abiding life with God. Jesus promises that if we abide in Him and He in us there will be an automatic result of great fruitfulness in and through our lives. But while we will automatically *bear much fruit* if we abide, we do not automatically *abide!* Authentic abiding requires serious intention and effort on our part. John 15:5 is a conditional, or covenantal, promise. Jesus proclaims, "*If* we abide in him..." God's part is to supernaturally produce fruit in and through our lives. Our part is to do whatever is required to remain in Him...to abide in His powerful, loving and holy presence.

For a discipleship plan to deliver sustained transformational impact, it must be intentional, holistic and thoroughly relational. Such a plan must:

- Address the past failures and pain that can hinder the disciple's vision and momentum with regard to the goal that God has marked out for them. *"Therefore, since we are surrounded by such a great cloud of witnesses, let us throw off everything that hinders and the sin that so easily entangles. And let us run with perseverance the race marked out for us, fixing our eyes on Jesus, the pioneer and perfecter of faith"* (Hebrews 12:1,2).

- It must help the disciple develop a spiritual lifestyle where he or she learns to practice the presence of God. *"I keep my eyes always on the Lord. With him at my right hand, I will not be shaken. Therefore my heart is glad and my tongue rejoices; my body also will rest secure"* (Psalm 16:8,9).

- It must prepare the disciple to fulfill their mission. *"For we are God's handiwork, created in Christ Jesus to do good works, which God prepared in advance for us to do"* (Ephesians 2:10).

- It must equip the disciple to stand fast against the devil's schemes and overcome the dominion of darkness. *"Put on the full armor of God, so that you can take your stand against the devil's schemes. For our struggle is not against flesh and blood, but against the rulers, against the authorities, against the powers of this dark world and against the spiritual forces of evil in the heavenly realms"* (Ephesians 6:11,12).

- And it must orient the disciple to do all the above in the context of tangible relationship with supportive friends. *"And let us consider how we may spur one another on toward love and good deeds, not giving up meeting together, as some are in the habit of doing, but encouraging one another—and all the more as you see the Day approaching"* (Hebrews 10:24,25).

The sad truth is that many believers tend to concentrate on their fruit bearing status rather than their relationship with the One who promises that we will automatically bear fruit if we would indeed abide. This unfortunate focus leads many into religious strife, legalism, hypocrisy, burn out and eventually spiritual despair. Re-focusing on the good news of the Kingdom and the commitments that can encourage an abiding life positions the disciple of Jesus to be the ongoing recipient and conduit of God's undeserved favor. In the following section, we will briefly explore this intentional focus as well as the kind of commitments and practices exhibited in Scripture and church history that serve to enable and encourage a consistent and fruitful life under the reign and rule of God. This framework can serve as a pathway to effective discipleship formation. A more detailed analysis of these areas will be offered throughout the pages of this book.

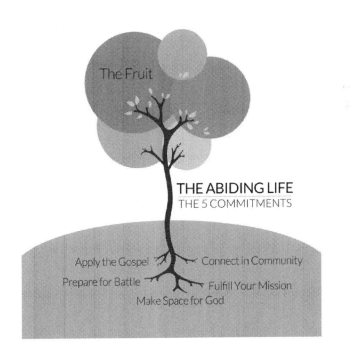

The Fruit

THE ABIDING LIFE
THE 5 COMMITMENTS

Apply the Gospel   Connect in Community
Prepare for Battle   Fulfill Your Mission
Make Space for God

THE COMMITMENTS THAT SUPPORT AN ABIDING LIFE:

Apply the gospel

Intentional focus should begin with *applying the gospel* to every reality of sin, brokenness and bondage in the believer's life. While there is abundant Gospel provision for every needful area of our lives, the efficacy of the Gospel is dependent upon our obedient response of faith. The application of the Good News is our responsibility and plays a vital role in securing and maintaining victory and stability in the Christian walk. Far too many believers fail to seriously and persistently apply the grace

> *To our sin the gospel offers forgiveness.*
> *To our sickness the gospel offers healing.*
> *To our sadness the gospel offers comfort.*
> *To our stuckness the gospel offers freedom.*
> *To our suffering the gospel offers hope.*

of the gospel to the areas of need in their lives. We simply have not learned to do so. In the following chapters I will describe how this pertains to facing the hindrances of sin, sickness, sadness and "stuckness" with the truth and power of God. And what about those who are not healed or set free through effective, compassionate prayer? Is there Good News for the suffering? Thankfully, because of God's Kingdom that has come and is coming, there is!

Make space for God

Intentionally developing good spiritual habits is also critical for fruitful living. Such practices as solitude, silence, Bible reflection, prayer and worship can serve to create space for God to work in and through the disciple. These disciplines can enlarge the disciple's capacity to know, obey and abide with God in a greater way. Healthy spiritual habits foster an atmosphere where God's voice and presence can be more readily experienced, enabling the believer to take hold of that which Christ has put within their reach.

Fulfill your mission

Beyond the commitment to apply the gospel and make space for God, followers of Christ must humbly and courageously seek to fulfill their role in the mission of God. Jesus exhorts those who have received his gracious message and ministry saying, "Freely you have received, freely give" (Matthew 10:8). It is imperative that Christ's followers believe that they were made on purpose and for a purpose. The Great Commission clarifies that Jesus' idea of discipleship is by definition "missional," when he commands that we, "Go and make disciples of all nations." This essentially links the concept of what it means to be and make a disciple with that of connecting with the "not-yets" of the world.[27] The possibility of a "missionless disciple" would be unthinkable to Jesus and his early followers. Yet today it appears that caring for the least and the lost is merely an optional activity on the discipleship menu.

Disciples need to know and appreciate how God has uniquely designed them in order to fulfill the Kingdom mission he has prepared for them. A lack of holistic self-awareness is not uncommon for believers, and provides a serious handicap for effective Kingdom living. Such understanding is critical for personal development as well as for healthy development and collaborative effectiveness when working with teams. Yet most disciples need more courage – not more information – to begin living in light of such truths. Courageous obedience to God's Word and the leading of God's Spirit, in tangible relationship with other believers committed to the same, is critical for the disciple who desires to cooperate in the mission of God.

Prepare for battle

Every sincere disciple must also quickly learn to be prepared for the inevitable opposition in the spiritual realm to the intention to abide

---

[27] Hugh Halter, *Sacrilege: Finding Life in the Unorthodox Ways of Jesus.* Baker Books, 2011. See the preface by Alan Hirsch for more on this.

with God and advance his Kingdom. The apostle Paul refers to this reality as spiritual warfare (cf., Ephesians 6:10ff.). As learning how to stand fast against the devil's schemes and to set the captives free was a clear emphasis in the training of Jesus' first followers, so should it be in ours. The Scriptures have much to say about spiritual strongholds and the possibility of demonization. A fruitful disciple who desires to live the life that Jesus has made possible must be functionally aware of and ready to deal with such things. Each of the six pieces of armor described in Ephesians 6 is strategically designed to cover an area that is highly vulnerable to the "Devil's schemes." The invitation to follow Jesus and advance his Kingdom is simultaneously a call to spiritual conflict. Therefore, it is imperative for the believer to appreciate the reality of the spiritual arena and to learn what it means to prayerfully put on the full armor of God.

Connect with supportive friends

Finally, disciples need to tangibly connect with supportive friends in the community of the King in order to embrace and sustain the life that Jesus has made possible. Connecting with others to support the decision to live under the rule of God is an essential means of grace. The Scriptures are very clear on this matter. Yet such connecting seldom occurs without serious intention and effort. As awkward and painful as community can be, little else promotes stability in Kingdom living like intentional Christian community.

THE PROMISE OF POWER!

The life Jesus has called his followers to requires the activation of his supernatural presence in our daily lives. Such spiritual power has been promised to every true disciple. This is power with a purpose as described in Acts 1:8, where Jesus told his first followers, "But you will receive power when the Holy Spirit comes upon you, and you will be my witnesses in Jerusalem, and in all Judea and Samaria and to the ends of the earth." We have not been commissioned to initiate ministry endeavors and then afterwards ask God to bless them, even though many believers seem to operate this way. God appreciates what he initiates, and he has promised to anoint what he appoints. Even Jesus lived in light of this truth. He testified that he could do nothing on his own (cf., John 5:30). It only makes sense that this principle would apply all the more to us, as Jesus revealed in John 15:5; "Apart from me you can do nothing." Sure, we can work hard and be very busy doing a variety of things, even religious things. But we will never be able to become or do anything that cannot be explained apart from God without the power of God at work in and through us.

Perhaps it's time for many of us to confess the truth of our spiritually impotent lives and ministries. The lack of God's transforming presence, which produces the fruit of true discipleship, explains why so many churches are barely surviving and why so many ministries are often described as ineffective, irrelevant and boring. Yet even in many churches that appear to be thriving there is a growing desire among its constituents for something more than exceptional programming. Though it is not always articulated this way, God's people want to intimately know Jesus and experience his manifest presence in and through their daily lives. They were designed for this sort of life. They want and desperately need all that God has provided to fulfill and transform their lives. This God-instilled hunger cannot be satisfied by anything or anyone else. The apostle Paul wrote to the Corinthian believers; "My message and my preaching were not with wise and persuasive words, but with a demonstration of the Spirit's power, so that your faith might not rest on men's wisdom, but on God's power" (1 Corinthians 2:4,5). Jesus invites every disciple to abide in his love, truth and power. Then with his empowering presence he leads us to go forth and transform the world! The Good News of the Kingdom changes everything, "For the Kingdom of God is not a matter of talk but of power" (1 Corinthians 4:20). It's time to explore and experience the Kingdom within our reach through a revolution of empowered discipleship! And this is where we are going in the following chapter.

CONCLUSION

Perhaps the greatest need today is for a courage awakening. We need courage to examine the temperature of our own personal discipleship; courage for leaders to honestly evaluate the progress toward Christ-likeness of those they lead; courage to embrace once again the face-to-face task of discipleship that has largely been outsourced to predigested classroom style programs, campus ministries, and Christian colleges and seminaries. How is it that so many churches are distracted from the one essential and clear thing we were told to do by Jesus? And when the obvious need for formation becomes apparent to us, how is it we don't know where to turn? Sadly, the church forgets how to do what it outsources.

Recent research on the American church reveals that for all our technological advances and programmatic savvy, people are not functionally becoming freer or courageously obedient in following Jesus.[28] No matter how sophisticated or cool, no consumeristic cure will be able to replace the life on life adventure of saying to another, "Follow me as I follow Christ" (1 Cor. 11:1).

---

[28] See for example the Willow Creek study called, *"Reveal: Where are you?"* by Greg L. Hawkins and Cally Parkinson, Willow Creek Resources.

CHAPTER 3

EMPOWERED BY THE SPIRIT

"But you will receive power when the Holy Spirit comes on you…"

- Jesus

Years ago, a family from our church made an appointment to talk with me about their decision to leave our congregation. This happened during a season when the Holy Spirit was moving in extraordinary ways in our gatherings. When I asked them exactly why they were leaving, they replied, "We don't feel comfortable with so much emphasis on the Kingdom and the ministry of the Spirit. We want to attend a church where the Word of God is the primary emphasis." After some discussion, we sadly said our goodbyes and I blessed them as they left my office.

To my surprise, another family had scheduled an appointment later that week to meet and announce that they, too, were leaving our church. As you might imagine, I wasn't looking forward to that conversation, but as we talked, they didn't share what I expected. Rather, they said they were frustrated that we weren't talking more about the Holy Spirit and delving more deeply into the supernatural elements of the gospel. They felt that spending such a large portion of our service on the expository preaching and teaching of the Bible was limiting what the Lord wanted to do in our midst.

I couldn't believe what I was hearing! It seemed like both families wanted us to choose between being a "truth" or a "power" church. But God calls his disciples to embrace both the truth of his Word *and* the power of His Spirit—both are essential ingredients for living the life Jesus made possible. No doubt, we will need to rely on God's wisdom and exercise courage to remain faithful to this critical balance taught and illustrated in Scripture

The example of Jesus and the early church is unquestionably a blended concert of truth and power as the gospel is proclaimed. Unfortunately, that is often not the case today. The fact is, the truth of God's Word points Jesus' followers to his power, and the Spirit, who is the power of God, always beacons them back to his truth. We never witness a contradiction or polarization of these two in the biblical narratives. This is well illustrated in the story of Paul's apostolic endeavor to plant a Kingdom outpost in Ephesus, a major Roman city at the time. Paul's third missionary tour launched him from his base in Antioch and took him through Galatia to the border of the great city of Ephesus.

REACHING A CITY FOR GOD

I imagine Paul had mixed feelings as he stood overlooking this epic metropolis. He had already faced persecution and spiritual warfare in city after city as he labored to advance God's Kingdom. And he certainly must have expected the same in a place like Ephesus, which was made famous by the cult of Diana and the great Temple of Artemis. This sophisticated organization of idolatry had heavily influenced the political, economic, and religious culture of the Ephesian community. People travelled from all over the world to admire and experience the impressive Temple, one of the great wonders of the world at that time.

As Paul peered over the skyline—with its world-renowned architectural masterpieces framing the horizon—he must have prayed and calculated the difficulty that lie ahead. Indeed, Ephesus would prove to be a city with demonic structures that opposed the good news of Jesus and the Kingdom of God. I imagine the apostle's heart was profoundly burdened by the realization that the Ephesians desperately needed to experience the life Jesus made possible. So, against all human odds, Paul made his way into the city limits determined to take this place for God. Here's how Paul's work began:

> There he found some disciples and asked them, "Did you receive the Holy Spirit when you believed?" They answered, "No, we have not even heard that there is a Holy Spirit." So Paul asked, "Then what baptism did you receive?" "John's baptism," they replied. Paul said, "John's baptism was a baptism of repentance. He told the people to believe in the one coming after him, that is, in Jesus" (Acts 19:1-4).

This is a fascinating story. Paul was aware of the eternal significance and potential danger of his task in Ephesus, and his first question reveals exactly where he placed his hope for a successful mission: "Did you receive the Holy Spirit when you believed? (v. 2). Paul undeniably knew that to successfully make disciples and advance God's Kingdom in Ephesus, he and his team would need to be totally dependent on Jesus and possess the supernatural power he promised (see Acts 1:8). Being clear of his mission made this a first-order question. Nothing could be more important than for Paul to know that these men's lives were empowered by the anointing of God.

It's interesting to note that in the Greek, the word "when" in Acts 19:2 can also be translated, "after." In other words, when Paul asked, "Did you receive the Holy Spirit when [after] you believed?", he was finding out if something definite had happened to them, something they would clearly know had taken place. He wasn't asking if something had happened that they might wonder about, guess at, or claim by faith. Indeed, if that had been the case, his question would have been absurd. Paul expected these disciples to be certain they had or had not been anointed with the power Jesus promised before he ascended to heaven (see Acts 1). Paul's question was obviously his starting point because this power made all the difference in the success or failure in his mission.

Today when those of us who follow Jesus experience God's empowering presence "when or after" we believe, we, too, will know this has happened in our lives. We won't have to wonder, guess, or claim it by faith. Having tangible evidence (or assurance) that we have received God's Spirit directly affects our confidence in ministering to others in God's power. Sadly, when desiring to advance God's Kingdom today, the first questions we often ask surrounds such issues as adequate funding, strategic facilities and creative programming.

I once sat in a church-planting meeting where the district leader suggested that if we'd all use the items listed in his newly assembled church planting toolkit, we would have a large church in no time. He actually called it an "instant church." But not one "tool" had anything to do with spiritual dependence, desperation, or anointing. Instead it was a clever advertising campaign with a bunch of programmatic ideas. The apostle Paul would have been outraged. Yet the all-too-common frenzy for ministry success can allow the multi-million-dollar resource industries to distract the Church from the most important ingredient in the advancement of God's Kingdom—the manifest presence of his Spirit! Resources and strategies are good, but they are only useful when they complement the leading and empowering presence of God. Without the Holy Spirit's power at work in and through our lives our labor will be in vain—no matter what resources we use.

I imagine Paul was utterly amazed when the disciples responded to him, "No, we have not even heard there is a Holy Spirit." Paul soon discovered that these followers had only been baptized by John, which was a baptism of preparation for a relationship with Jesus—the Messiah for whom they had been waiting. Realizing that they were prepared but not converted, Paul explained the gospel to them and then proceeded to re-baptize these newly born-again believers. The text goes on to say:

> On hearing this, they were baptized in the name of
> the Lord Jesus. When Paul placed his hands on them,
> the Holy Spirit came on them, and they spoke in
> tongues and prophesied. There were about twelve men
> in all. (Acts 19:5-7)

When these men came up out of the water Paul placed his hands on them and the Spirit fell upon them unleashing God's manifest presence and gracing them with supernatural gifts. These twelve men were transformed from being disciples of John to being Spirit-anointed followers of Jesus. This is the kind of person the apostle wanted on his team: disciples of Jesus who were anointed with power from on high!

THE HOLY SPIRIT *IN* AND *UPON* YOU!

Most evangelicals have an adequate theology of the Holy Spirit's role in conversion and sanctification, but many have an inadequate appreciation for the critical work of the Spirit to empower believers today for Kingdom ministry. It is helpful to reflect on the different prepositions used to describe the work of the Spirit.

In Scripture, we see the Spirit coming *IN* and *UPON* followers of Jesus. It is the Spirit's ministry *in* us that regenerates us and causes us to be born again. Jesus teaches this when speaking to Nicodemus says: "I tell you the truth, no one can enter the kingdom of God unless he is born of water and the Spirit. Flesh gives birth to flesh, but the Spirit gives birth to Spirit" (John 3:5,6). Paul made this clear in Romans 8:9 where he said that no one could be a child of God without the Spirit of God within them. It is also the Spirit's work *in* us, which begins at conversion, that activates the sanctifying process of making us more like Jesus. But it is the Spirit's work *upon* us that unleashes the supernatural power of God in and through our lives.

As Jesus said, "You will receive power when the Holy Spirit comes *upon* you...." (Acts 1:8). Here Jesus was promising his power to those who had already been born again. These disciples were with Jesus forty days earlier on the evening of his resurrection when he breathed on them and said, "Receive the Holy Spirit" (John 20:22). They had the Spirit *in* them for conversion, but not *upon* them for power.[29] That would not happen until fifty days later, on the day of Pentecost.

Rather than send off the disciples immediately into their missional destiny (cf., Matthew 28:18-20; Luke 24:46-49), they were told to wait for the promise of power to be unleashed on their lives (cf., Acts 1:4-5). During the forty days of Jesus' resurrection presence on earth, he spoke to his disciples about the Kingdom of God (cf., Acts 1:3). This is what Jesus had spoken of and demonstrated throughout his earthly ministry. Now he was delegating the ministry of the Kingdom to his followers. Jesus knew they would need Kingdom power for an authentic Kingdom ministry. The disciples took Jesus at his word, and the promise of power became the focus of a ten-day prayer meeting (cf., Acts 1:14), which epically concluded on the day of Pentecost when God poured out his Holy Spirit upon those praying believers.

Let us not miss the pattern illustrated here: It moves from the promise, to prayer, to Pentecost! We must recover this pattern today in our efforts to serve Jesus and advance his Kingdom, both in our neighborhoods and the nations abroad. Just like the ministry of the first disciples, so Paul's work in Ephesus had to wait until his team was anointed with power. And when the Spirit came upon them, there was no doubt that the same Spirit that was *in* them for conversion was now *on* them for an empowered ministry. The thriving church that grew out of Paul's ministry demonstrates the importance of this Kingdom dynamic.

---

[29] This same condition is found among some new believers in Samaria who came to faith through the preaching of Philip (Acts 8:12). On hearing of this missional breakthrough, the apostles in Jerusalem sent Peter and John to investigate. Luke goes on to describe: "When they arrived they prayed for them that they might receive the Holy Spirit, because the Holy Spirit had not yet come *upon* any of them..." (Acts 8:15,16).

WHAT ABOUT SPEAKING IN TONGUES?

The twelve disciples Paul baptized in Ephesus both spoke in tongues and prophesied when they were bathed in the empowering presence of God. Since the first century, some Christians have claimed that speaking in tongues is Jesus' exclusive signature of approval that a person has been baptized in the Spirit's power. Yet the apostle Paul corrected the church in Corinth on this misguided notion (see 1 Corinthians 12-14). While tongues can be, and often is, an accompanying experience for believers who are filled with the Spirit, this is not always the case (note: Paul asks in 1 Cor. 12:30, "Do all have gifts of healing? Do all speak in tongues? Do all interpret?" And the implied answer is, 'No!').

Unfortunately, throughout time the pendulum has swung widely regarding the spiritual gift of tongues. Once while in college, a friend told me that she doubted my salvation simply because I had not yet spoken in tongues. At the same time, I could recall hearing repeated, strong warnings by my well-meaning youth group ministry staff regarding the dangers of speaking in tongues. As a relatively new believer, I quickly encountered the Word vs. Spirit dilemma.

Today I deeply appreciate the apostle Paul's perspective who testified that he loved his gift of tongues, but would gladly lay it down if it might confuse or distract someone from the reality of Jesus. I believe followers of Christ should positively appreciate this manifestation of God, yet never make it a major agenda item or a badge of spiritual superiority. It's unfortunate that many today actually fear this spiritual gifting, along with other manifestations of the Holy Spirit that they are unfamiliar with. Could it be that when we say "no" to the manifestations of God, we are also saying "no" to his empowering presence? In truth, it simply isn't wise to put limits on how God can and cannot perform his supernatural work in and through our lives!

THERE MUST BE MORE!

After marrying my college sweetheart, we moved to Massachusetts, where I attended Gordon-Conwell Theological Seminary. I loved my classes, but soon developed an ache in my soul for something more than simply gaining biblical and theological knowledge. I knew something was missing, and this realization only became clearer the more I examined Scripture. I loved God and had even been privileged through the years to lead many into a relationship with Jesus. But I knew that something significant was lacking in my life with him. This led me to desperately seek the Lord each morning before school.

Finally, after my last exam in December, I made my way from the lecture hall to the library where I was determined to find direction about being filled with the Holy Spirit. I decided to look for a relevant sermon or lecture series in the library archives. After some searching, I found a presentation by the Charismatic Renewal Movement of the Presbyterian Church U.S.A. on the Baptism of the Holy Spirit. Being Presbyterian at the time, I thought this was a safe place to begin, even though I recall looking around to make sure no one saw me checking out that particular message!

Once home, I hurriedly went into our living room to listen to the message, which was a simple unfolding of some Scriptures and comments primarily from the Book of Acts. Then the speaker said, "Please bow your heads now and let's ask the Spirit to come upon us." And so I got down on my knees and began praying. To my surprise, I experienced something I had never felt before: I felt like a powerful flow of tingling warmth was being poured out all over my body. It was as though God was soaking and filling me with a river of liquid love. All I could do was cry out in praise and thanksgiving.

After several minutes, I ran out of words to express my appreciation. I wanted to keep thanking God and glorifying him, but I'd said everything I knew to say. Then suddenly God gave me more words to proclaim my love for him, though now I was speaking in a language I had never learned. I'm not sure how long this went on, but when I finally was able to stand up, I was different. A supernatural change had occurred in me from the inside out. Now, when I read and studied the bible, its message had somehow become more alive. Worship became more intimate. I found myself sharing my faith with more passion and boldness. And when I prayed for people, I began to consistently see things happen that were new to my ministry experience.

A few years later, my friend Ron Malionek and I traveled to a conference in Southern California featuring John Wimber and Blaine Cook. Having heard stories of Wimber's ministry in the Vineyard, we were curious about what we might experience. The first session of the conference began with an extended time of intimate worship. John then stepped up on stage and began teaching about Jesus and the Kingdom he ushered into the world. His message was intriguing—making Jesus seem very relevant and real. That day the Kingdom became clearly tangible to me, a reality I could readily embrace. At the end of each session John would simply pray, "Come, Holy Spirit." And session after session, I saw the power of God fall upon those gathered. John and Blaine offered numerous "words of knowledge" that revealed specific conditions of people in the audience. As the ministry team prayed for those desiring prayer, we witnessed many people getting healed and others being set free of demonic oppression. This was a game changer for me. There would be no turning back! I was finally witnessing what I had personally encountered in my living room, but had never experienced in a gathered community.

Back at home, we gathered a core group of friends and excitedly shared our stories. After teaching from the Word about our need for the Spirit's power to advance God's Kingdom, I said, "I don't know what else to do, except I'm pretty sure we should just pray and ask God to touch us with his presence." After a few minutes of prayer and waiting silently, I noticed one man's hand starting to tremble. Soon his whole body was shaking. This was a man I knew well. He was someone who valued self-control—a person I was sure would only be shaking if the Spirit was touching him. Then a woman began to weep. Strangely, the man sitting next to her started to giggle, which gradually grew into an unstoppable roar of laughter. After a few minutes, all but one of us had experienced some kind of visible manifestation of the Spirit's presence, which went on for some time before a wonderful outpouring of peace filled the room.

As we debriefed what had happened, there was great joy in sharing how God had touched us in such personal and powerful ways. I felt badly for the one man who hadn't expressed any visible manifestations, so I hesitantly asked him, "How are you doing?" to which he responded, "That was the most powerful encounter with God I've ever had!" No tongues. No shaking or crying or laughing. But he was changed forever by the love and power of God that had quietly fallen on him that night with no visible indications from our perspective.

That night we all experienced something different. God did not touch any of us in exactly the same way, yet each of us received what we needed. Afterward, we noticed a deepening sense of God's presence in worship, a new capacity to pray for the sick and see people healed, and a boldness to share our faith with neighbors, coworkers and friends. To say the least, our little church took off in new ways. In the years to come we would see many conversions, healings and deliverances. We were followers of Jesus who were hungry for the Word and thirsty for the Spirit. By God's grace we had become a bona fide truth and power church!

The reality is that some form of what I have just shared can happen for anyone who hungers for the Word and thirsts for the Spirit. Through the years, I've personally witnessed this supernatural encounter radically impacting countless individuals and groups—both large and small. And I'm convinced that Jesus' declaration, "You will receive power when the Holy Spirit comes upon you," is not a time bound promise meant only for the early church, but something intended for all of us, a reality urgently needed by those who desire to live the life Jesus made possible.

REVIVE US AGAIN, LORD!

Yes, it's true: the Holy Spirit is still touching, filling, and baptizing people—today. And yet one of the disappointing realities of being filled with God's Spirit is that *we leak*. In other words, yesterday's anointing will not guarantee today's success in life or in the advancement of the Kingdom. The early church certainly understood this. The same disciples who were anointed with power on the day of Pentecost are found again, just two chapters later in the Book of Acts, crying out to God in an upper room:

> *Pentecost wasn't the end but rather the beginning of a new lifestyle informed by the power of God.*

> Now, Lord, consider their threats and enable your servants to speak your word with great boldness. Stretch out your hand to heal and perform signs and wonders through the name of your holy servant Jesus." After they prayed, the place where they were meeting was shaken. And they were all filled with the Holy Spirit and spoke the word of God boldly. (Acts 4:29-31)

Pentecost wasn't the end but rather the beginning of a new lifestyle informed by the power of God. Yet, unfortunately, it's possible for people to have a dramatic encounter with God's love, truth, and power, then live as if that were an isolated historical fact. Some people become fixated upon the date they came to Christ, or the manifestation they experienced when they were first filled with his Spirit. But making any point in time an end in itself is not God's desire for us. We must abide in him moment by moment, remaining humble and hungry for more of his Spirit every day. We have to learn what it means to "fan into flame the gift of God" (2 Timothy 1:6), and keep ourselves burning brightly for his glory as we seek the advance of his Kingdom. That is why "revival" remains such an important focus for the church today. Richard Lovelace underscores this point in his summary of Jonathon Edwards' views on revival:

> Revival…is an outpouring of the Holy Spirit which restores the people of God to normal spiritual life after a period of corporate declension. Periods of spiritual decline occur in history because the gravity of indwelling sin keeps pulling believers first into formal religion and then into open apostasy. Periods of awakening alternate with these as God graciously breathes new life into his people. Every major advance of the kingdom of God on earth is signaled and brought about by a general outpouring of the Holy Spirit.[30]

Lovelace's quote emphasizes the truth that a personal or corporate encounter with God's renewing presence is essential, yet it is not an end in itself. God pours out his Spirit again and again with the purpose of renewing and empowering believers for his glory, for transformation, and for the sake of fulfilling their missional destiny.

SEEKING HIS KINGDOM FIRST!

After the apostle Paul saw his team empowered by God's Spirit in Ephesus, he headed to the local synagogue where he "spoke boldly… for three months, arguing persuasively about the kingdom of God" (Acts 19:8).

In emphasizing the Kingdom of God, Paul was following the example Jesus set throughout his earthly ministry. In fact, the subject of the Kingdom was a primary focus of Jesus' discussions with his disciples during his last forty days on earth between the resurrection

---

[30] Richard Lovelace, *Dynamics of Spiritual Life: An Evangelical Theology of Renewal* (Downers Grove, IL: IVP, 1979), p. 40.

and the ascension (see Acts 1:3). It was to remain their priority, and it is to be ours as well.

As described in chapter one of this book, the Kingdom of God refers to the functional rule of God. The mission of the Church that Jesus would build through his disciples was to advance God's Kingdom (cf., Matthew 16:18-19). Today we are still meant to declare and demonstrate the reality of the Kingdom come and coming, "making all things new" (Revelation 21:5). Paul kept the Kingdom central in his ministry to his dying day as we learn from the last verse in the Book of Acts; "Boldly and without hindrance he (Paul) preached the Kingdom of God and taught about the Lord Jesus Christ" (Acts 28:31). We too must continue to boldly proclaim God's reign and rule in both word and deed. To be faithful and fruitful in what matters to God, we must maintain this ministry focus. And having missional clarity regarding our commission to advance the Kingdom only underscores our desperate need for Kingdom power, unless we are satisfied with offering a truncated gospel that offers little more than programs and tools.

Conversions, healings, and deliverances became the persuasive components of Paul's ministry, launching a transformational movement in the city of Ephesus. This message and ministry of the Kingdom were good news to many, but not all. As the word of the Lord "spread widely and grew in power" (Acts 19:20), so did opposition to the advancement of the gospel movement. Paul's opponents included Jews who refused to believe his message (see Acts 19:9), as well a group of city businessmen who profited by crafting and selling artifacts in honor of the cult of Artemis (see Acts 19:23ff). Yet the disciples in Ephesus were "overcoming evil with good" (see Romans 12:21), systemically driving the cult out of business. For Paul and others who desire to see God's Kingdom come, one must be prepared for the inevitable rhythm of "battle/ breakthrough ...breakthrough/ battle," because the devil doesn't give up ground without a fight!

TRUTH AND POWER: WE DON'T HAVE TO CHOOSE!

When the atmosphere turned negative for Paul at the synagogue in Ephesus, his apostolic instinct was to establish a new ministry base in a rented lecture hall:

> Paul entered the synagogue and spoke boldly there for three months, arguing persuasively about the kingdom of God. But some of them became obstinate; they refused to believe and publicly maligned the Way. So, Paul left them. He took the disciples with him and had discussions daily in the lecture hall of Tyrannus. This went on for two years, so that all the Jews and Greeks who lived in the province of Asia heard the word of the Lord. (Acts 19:8-10)

Clearly the lecture hall of Tyrannus became the new facility where an apostolic band of disciples were equipped to take the gospel throughout all of Asia Minor. This was a two-year intensive training program where Paul was likely teaching the Scriptures with an emphasis on Jesus and the theological and practical implications of his Kingdom now within our reach.[31] Paul held a very high view of Scripture—valuing the importance of teaching it to others for spiritual transformation. This is clear from his instruction to Timothy, who years later was appointed by Paul to lead the church in Ephesus, "All Scripture is God-breathed and is useful for teaching, rebuking, correcting and training in righteousness, so that the servant of God may be thoroughly equipped for every good work" (2 Timothy 3:16-17). Missional clarity and the power of the Holy Spirit to carry out that mission is essential, yet without a growing biblical foundation, a

---

[31] The emphasis in Paul's teaching on Jesus and the Kingdom is found throughout Paul's letters and the book of Acts. It is succinctly summarized in the last verse of Acts: "Boldly and without hindrance he preached the kingdom of God and taught about the Lord Jesus Christ" (Acts 28:31).

Christian work and its workers will lack authentic spiritual authority and be vulnerable to error.

History has repeatedly demonstrated that biblical/theological illiteracy eventually contributes to ministry dysfunction and leadership failures of all kinds. Paul's ingenious strategy was to intensely equip his emerging leaders in a relatively short amount of time, then commission them into the harvest. The apostle knew it was essential that the disciples learn how to study the bible on his or her own[32] while also being dependent on the Spirit.[33] They would need to take what they had learned and immediately give it to others who would be faithful to give it away to others still.[34] Without these basic disciplines in place, there will never be a sustained Kingdom movement.

All this to say, it is crucial to maintain a dynamic balance between a continuous focus on the truth of God's Word and the power of his Spirit. This may sound simple and obvious, but Evangelicals and Charismatics have historically had difficulty doing this.[35] There is something right and essential about embracing a disciplined approach to the study of God's Word coupled with a commitment to the supernatural ministry of the Holy Spirit. Again, it is imperative to engage mission with a balance of truth *and* power. We don't have to choose, in fact, we must NOT choose. One without the other is like running a race on only one leg. Evangelicals and Charismatics need to be sincerely open to one another and humbly learn from the other with respect. Ken Wilson summarizes this well when he writes:

> If we emphasize the Word without the Spirit, we *dry up*. If we emphasize the Spirit without the Word, we

---

[32] 2 Timothy 2:15 – "Study to show thyself approved unto God, a workman that needs not to be ashamed, rightly dividing the word of truth" (KJV).

[33] 2 Timothy 1:6

[34] 2 Timothy 2:2

[35] A few years ago, I received an email from Dr. Gary Benedict, a previous president of the movement I have been associated with that included this telling observation: "The person and work of the Holy Spirit is central to our C&MA history, yet now often neglected because of fear of Charismatics, excesses, and false teaching."

blow up. If we hold the Word and the Spirit together, we *grow up.* We won't gain more of the Spirit by having less of the Word. And we won't depend less on the Word by having more of the Spirit. We need as much of both as we can have.[36]

> *It takes a truth and power church made up of disciples who both hunger for the Word and thirst for the Spirit to transform the world in Jesus' name.*

As Paul emphasized both the ministry of the Spirit and the Word, he demonstrated how an intentional theological formation was necessary to equip the saints for ministry. Luke mentions that all the Jews and Greeks who lived in the province of Asia heard the word of the Lord because Paul held daily discussions in the lecture hall of Tyrannus for two years (Acts 19:10). This sounds more like Paul was having a bible study than a revival meeting. Yet in the very next verse, Luke records, "God did extraordinary miracles through Paul,[37] where divine healings and deliverances occurred (Acts 19:11). It is obvious that serious study of God's Word, along with supernatural ministry, were both happening in the same season. Luke summarizes this scenario with, "In this way the word of the Lord spread widely and grew in power" (Acts 19:20). It takes a truth *and* power church made up of

---

[36] Nathan, Rich; Wilson, Ken (2009-07-07). *Empowered Evangelicals* (Kindle Locations 585-588). Ampelon Publishing. Kindle Edition.

[37] I have often wondered what an "ordinary miracle" would be. It likely would include such things as divine healing, deliverance, and raising the dead. The fact that Luke testifies that God was doing extraordinary miracles through the apostle Paul means that there was no precedent for such manifestations. God was choosing to do something new. It might even be appropriately called an "extra-biblical" manifestation. No one would have been able to answer the question so often asked today, "Now where is that in the bible?" It is imperative for us to appreciate the essential difference between extra-biblical and contra-biblical. I believe we must remain cautiously open to the possibility of an extra-biblical manifestation of God, yet remain resolutely opposed to anything contra-biblical. Here is one important reason why the gift of discernment is critical for a community of truth and power disciples. As the apostle Paul wrote to the Thessalonians with regard to an occasion when God may have said or done something extraordinary, we too must not automatically reject or accept such things. Rather, we must, "Test everything. Hold on to the good. Avoid every kind of evil" (1 Thessalonians 5:21-22).

disciples who both hunger for the Word *and* thirst for the Spirit to transform the world in Jesus' name.

CONCLUSION

Personally, I want to live a life that cannot be explained apart from the reality of a Risen King who is supernaturally at work in and through me. I want to give myself to a ministry that bears testimony to the truth that Jesus is alive and is the same yesterday, today, and forever (see Hebrews 13:8). And I'm certain that I am not alone in this! Yet this desire can never become a reality without a commitment to openness and a dependency on the manifest presence of God in our lives. To exclude the supernatural work of the Spirit is to settle for something less than the life Jesus made possible. Francis Chan articulates this passionately when he writes:

> You don't need the Holy Spirit if you are merely seeking to live a semi-moral life and attend church regularly. You can find people of all sorts in many religions doing that quite nicely without Him. You only need the Holy Spirit's guidance and help if you truly want to follow the Way of Jesus Christ. You only need Him if you desire to "obey everything" He commanded and to teach others to do the same (Matt. 28:18-20 NIV). You only need the Holy Spirit if you have genuinely repented and believe. And you only need the Holy Spirit if you understand that you are called to share in Christ's suffering and death, as well as His resurrection (Rom. 8:17; 2 Cor. 4:16-18; Phil. 3:10-11).[38]

---

[38] Francis Chan. *Forgotten God: Reversing Our Tragic Neglect of the Holy Spirit* (Kindle Locations 838-842). Kindle Edition.

My prayerful hope is that this chapter has captured your attention regarding a daunting need in the church today and has inspired a personal thirst for the Spirit that will turn into a relentless quest in your own heart before the Lord. I end this chapter with this epic promise from Jesus:

> If you then, though you are evil, know how to give good gifts to your children, how much more will your Father in heaven give the Holy Spirit to those who ask him! (Luke 11:13)

What you sincerely desire will determine what you desperately ask God for.

PART 2

THE WHOLENESS JESUS MADE POSSIBLE

CHAPTER 4

PHYSICAL HEALING TODAY

"And the prayer offered in faith will make the sick person well;
the Lord will raise him up."

James 5:15

In 1982, after suffering from various symptoms for many years, I was finally diagnosed with hypoglycemia. My condition was verified during an extended glucose analysis, and that day the hospital dietician told me that I would need to be on a restricted diet the rest of my life. Hearing that—especially after an entire day of being poked with needles—was definitely *not* good news!

As a follower of Jesus, I certainly knew that God could heal me, and I had received prayer for my condition on numerous occasions. But the symptoms did not go away; in fact, my spells of dizziness and "brain fog" seemed to get worse. About six years after the diagnosis, I was visiting a large church when the pastor began encouraging people to gather in small groups to pray for the sick. He said confidently, "I believe God is going to touch people here who are suffering from hypoglycemia. If that's you, stand up because God wants to heal you." After all this time, you'd think I'd have jumped to my feet, eager to get prayer. But truthfully, my expectation to be healed had diminished drastically. Fortunately, my wife, Jill, extended the 'elbow of encouragement' until I finally stood up!

Then Jill and some friends gathered around me to pray. While the leader gave specific instructions, their prayers were heartfelt and unhurried. At first, I couldn't tell if anything was happening. But as they continued to pray, an unusual heat began to sweep across my body. By the time the prayer ended, I was soaking with perspiration, feeling exhausted and overwhelmed. Though not certain I was healed, I certainly knew that something powerful had just taken place.

In the days that followed, I experienced no further symptoms of the disease. And a few months later, I received medical verification that indeed my blood sugar levels were stable and normal. That was almost three decades ago, and to this day I've remained completely well. Yes, our Jesus is indeed the Mighty Healer!

GOD'S DESIRE TO HEAL

One thing we see in Scripture again and again is God's concern for the sick. Jesus showed that by healing people everywhere he went. As Matthew recorded, "Jesus went throughout Galilee, teaching in their synagogues, preaching the good news of the kingdom, and healing every disease and sickness among the people" (Matthew 4:23). Ministering to the sick was such a significant part of Jesus' ministry that nearly forty percent of the Gospel narratives deal with some aspect of healing. Jesus sought out the sick, giving those who suffered his special attention. No one can refute the fact that Jesus has always been tender toward those plagued by infirmity and disease.

Today Jesus' heart is still moved by the sick. The One who is the same yesterday, today, and forever (Hebrews 13:8) is still in the business of setting people free from all manner of sickness, brokenness, and bondage. He wants to heal us because he loves us, and when his love and power are displayed, he is glorified. The ministry of physical healing always has been and always will be a core component of the good news of Jesus Christ.

BY GRACE WE ARE HEALED

In any discussion of divine healing, it's important to begin by stating that healing, just like salvation, is accomplished by grace alone.

No one is healed—just like no one is saved—because they've earned it. The gospel accounts show that Jesus healed all kinds of people wherever he went; he didn't distinguish between those who were good and those who were not. This is important because many people believe that God heals (and does not heal) based on our personal merits. Therefore, when we feel unworthy, we struggle to trust that God will heal us. And that's why, for many of us, the question is not so much *can* God heal, but *will* He heal *me?* …or those *I* pray for? To mistakenly believe that God only heals those who deserve it will keep us from seeking healing in our own lives (which I have experienced), as well as praying for others.

Just like salvation, the good news is that God gives healing not as a reward for a life well lived, but as a free gift that flows out of his great mercy and love. We need to appreciate that the hurting are healed because of God's heart of compassion. God desires to touch all who humbly ask for his healing grace.

The man with leprosy found Jesus is willing to heal: "'If you are willing, you can make me clean.' And filled with compassion, Jesus reached out and touched the man, '*I am willing,*' he said. 'Be clean!'" (Mark 1:40-41). In the next verse we discover that Jesus is both *willing* and *able* to heal. "Immediately the leprosy left him and he was cured" (Mark 1:42). God is still willing and able to heal the sick today. This indeed is good news!

The same compassion of God that motivated Jesus to reach out to the leper is available to us today, only now Jesus' care is dispensed to the world through us—his servants. As God's representatives, we are the ones who currently take his healing to a needy world because we have been commissioned to do so. Our confidence in praying for sick includes the fact that the healing for humankind has been paid in full (see Isaiah 53:4-5; 1 Peter 2:21-24; Matthew 8:14-17). And Jesus, who is still willing and able to heal, has imparted to us the same spiritual power that he utilized in his earthly ministry (See Isaiah 61:1; Luke 4:18-21; John 14:12; 16:7; Acts 1:8). And because the Kingdom of God remains among us, it is not only our privilege but also our responsibility to advance his domain by healing the sick in partnership with him (see Matthew 12:28; Mark 1:15; Luke 17:21).

CONDITIONS CONDUCIVE TO DIVINE HEALING

We have already considered how Jesus placed God's Kingdom within our reach, and how the benefits of that Kingdom are now ours—here and now. This includes divine healing, which God has done *His part* to ensure. The question is, what is *our part* in seeing divine healing take place in our environment? A.B. Simpson writes:

> It [healing] is not a special gift of discriminating favoritism, but a great and common heritage of faith and obedience…. It is true that all who come must conform to the simple conditions of obedient faith. But these are impartial without respect of persons and within the reach of all who trust and obey.[39]

Even though God made healing available and commissioned us to extend that healing on earth, there are several key ingredients that make an environment more conducive for divine healing. These components create a platform upon which God's healing presence is more likely to manifest. However, we must remember that it is God who heals—not the arrangement of ideal conditions. No one can force God's hand; we are always humbly dependent on Him. That being said, the following factors do produce a more favorable climate through which God's Kingdom can advance.

---

[39] As quoted in *Healing Voices: A Narrative of the Acts of God in the Christian & Missionary Alliance.* Stephen Adams and K. Neill Foster (editors). (Camp Hill, PA: Christian Publications, Inc., 2000, 9.

Faith

One of the most important ingredients for divine healing is the exercise of Biblical faith. This faith is not mere intellectual assent but is the kind of trust that leads to surrender and active obedience. Mark's account in Nazareth highlights the importance of faith: "He [Jesus] could not do any miracles there, except lay his hands on a few sick people and heal them. And he was amazed at their lack of faith" (Mark 6:5-6). What a startling reality, Jesus himself was limited by an environment of unbelief!

When it comes to faith, it's important to clarify that faith itself does not heal. Faith is simply the channel through which divine healing flows. God heals *through* our faith in him. Misunderstanding the role of faith has led many to exhort those being prayed for to have greater faith. But healing is not about having more or better faith; healing comes from the *object* of our faith—God himself. Jesus promised, "I tell you the truth, anyone who has *faith in me* will do what I have been doing" (John 14:12).

Unfortunately, being told that one has not been healed because of a lack of faith has wounded many sincere saints in the body of Christ. Over the years, I have witnessed a number of 'faith healers' vigorously praying for God to move; but when healing didn't occur, some of those same 'healers' have left the one they were praying for in worse condition than before they had received any 'ministry'.

Years ago I was part of a ministry team that was invited to pray for the sick at a conference. I joined others who were praying for a woman in a wheelchair. This sweet lady had obviously been in that condition most of her life, as her legs and feet lay lifeless and withered in the chair. After several minutes of boisterous prayer and declarations, one man told the woman she needed to take off her shoes and stand up, to which she responded, "Oh no, I can't do that." The man replied that she would not be healed unless she did. Finally, she was persuaded to follow his instructions. With great effort she tried to stand, but it soon became clear that this was not going to happen. At that point, most of the ministry team transitioned quickly from praying for her to speaking impersonally about her with one another. One man eventually stated, "You just need to have more faith;" then he turned and left her sitting barefoot and alone in her chair.

Part of me wanted to have those folks arrested for spiritual abuse! But, refocusing my attention, I sat with the woman for a few moments before offering to help her put on her shoes. With tears streaming down her face, she shared how this was not the first time something like this had happened. I felt awkward yet somehow privileged to be listening to her story. As she spoke, I realized this was a real woman of faith, a warrior in the Kingdom of God. Perhaps like the apostle Paul whom the Lord allowed to live with a thorn in the flesh, this wounded disciple had been serving her Master from this wheelchair for a long time.

It's true that faith and healing are dynamically tied, but the person exercising the faith is often the pray-er rather than the pray-ee. There have been numerous times when the only faith a pray-ee seemed to have was that which brought them to me for prayer— but that was enough! I've discovered that faith often grows once a person encounters God's presence in the healing prayer encounter. The truth is that the size or quality of one's faith is not as significant as the fact that we are humbly exercising the faith that we've been given.

It must be said that even exercising the faith we have is not a guarantee that healing will result. It is not our faith that heals the sick, but rather God, who can work miraculously through our faith. That is why I prefer to call this gracious work of God 'divine healing' rather than 'faith healing'. It is the Person of Christ rather than our faith that heals. Therefore, a lack of faith for healing is really a lack of faith in the God who has promised and provided for this supernatural blessing. Christians in the western world tend to be especially challenged with this version of unbelief, because at least in part, we have so many medical options in which to put our trust. Rich Nathan makes an interesting point when he writes:

> Perhaps the 'lack of faith' in the western world in general, and our western churches in particular, explains why there seem to be fewer healings here than are reported in the other two-thirds of the world. While we tend to attribute the relative abundance of divine healings there to new church planting, or illiteracy, or their supposed need for the supernatural, it simply may boil down to greater faith in their communities and churches (see Matthew 8:5-13).[40]

Faith is simply the means by which we focus our hearts in humble confidence on our all-sufficient God. And as we do, our faith (not faith *in faith* but faith *in God*) functions as the channel through which healing can flow from our all-loving, all-powerful Savior.

Expectation

Another common and unfortunate misconception is with regard to the importance of expectation. While *faith* is related to our trust that God *can* heal, *expectation* relates to our trust that God *will* heal in a specific situation. Some rather passionately believe that when the sick receive prayer, we should not encourage them to expect divine healing from the Lord. I have been confronted more than once by a person who was offended because I teach people to pray for the sick with an expectant heart. One woman recently told me that encouraging people to expect that they will be healed only sets them up for disappointment when it doesn't happen. And what then, she asked, will that communicate about God? That might be a legitimate question that deserves some prayerful thought. Yet here's another question to consider. What might it testify about God if divine healing does occur

---

[40] Rich Nathan and Ken Wilson, *Empowered Evangelicals: Bringing Together the best of the Evangelical and Charismatic Worlds.* (Kindle edition, Ampelon Publishing, 2009), Kindle Locations 3396-3406

as a result of our praying for someone with expectation? The Scriptures are certainly not silent on this point.

> ### What is our expectation with regard to supernatural ministry?
>
> - Some would say, **"We should expect *nothing* to happen *all* of the time."** Our dispensational friends functionally embrace this view.
>
> - Others would say, **"We should expect *everything* to happen *all* of the time."** Our friends with an over-realized eschatology embrace this mindset. Heaven alone is where we can expect everything to happen all of the time.
>
> - We would say, **"We should expect *everything* to happen *some* of the time."** This is the occasional testimony of revival and extraordinary manifestations of the Holy Spirit since the days of the early church.
>
> - We would also say, **"We should expect *something* to happen *all of the time*."** This is our attitude as people who live under the influence of the Kingdom come and coming!

Clearly one's faith and expectation in divine healing (or lack thereof) influences if and how we pray for the sick. As Derek Morphew suggests, our doctrines of "dispensationalism and cessationism" have sadly reduced what we expect from God in the way of healing.[41] Truthfully, I believe the resistance to such prayer is not so much a theological issue for most people as it is a simple issue of fear and pride. Deciding *not* to pray for the sick ultimately becomes less about God (or even the person being prayed for) and more about us! "What might people say or think of me or of God if I pray for someone and they are not healed?" If we are honest with ourselves, avoiding this uncomfortable scenario is often our primary concern. Recently I heard

---

[41] Morphew, p. 97

someone say, "I am afraid that nothing will happen if I pray for the lump on my friend's back." And because of their fear that "nothing will happen" and the pride related to how this might look, prayer was not offered and obviously, there was no chance for healing prayer to be effective as it was avoided altogether. How sad.

Once again, the bottom line is that our faith is not in healing per se, but in the God who heals. We simply pray for the sick in humble confidence and obedience to Jesus' command to do so. And as we put our trust in God's loving presence, promises, and power, we then ask him with hopeful expectation to do what only he can do. That is how we obediently partner with the Almighty, expecting his healing presence to confront sickness and advance his Kingdom on earth.

Compassion

Another reason we pray for the sick is because we, like Jesus, are moved by their infirmities. In the gospel accounts when Jesus saw hurting people, their afflictions touched his heart (cf., Matthew 14:14). Whether Jesus was tired from feeding the multitudes or near death while hanging on a cross, he was always filled with compassionate grace. We would do well to grow in this attribute of Jesus as well. God's healing presence often flows through hearts that feel deep affection and are broken over other's pain. We often hear people say that they've

> *Sadly, ministry without compassion often turns hurting people into projects.*

felt God's tangible love while receiving prayer. Such love serves to drive out fear and opens the way for a healing encounter.

I had a dear friend who began experiencing serious back pain while on a ministry trip. She was in agony for days, and many people prayed for her. But when one young man, who was particularly fond of this lady, learned of her pain, he started to contend for her healing in prayer. She tried to stop him (since so many had already prayed), but he would not be dissuaded. His concern and compassion were genuine and strong, and even when she had no relief, he insisted on

accompanying her quite a distance to her room. The next morning when she awoke, her back was totally healed! Something happens in the spiritual realm when faith is activated by love (Galatians 5:6). And the truth is, the healing touch of Jesus consistently finds its motivation in a heart full of compassionate love. Sadly, ministry without compassion often turns hurting people into projects.

The Manifest Presence of God

One of the mysteries of the faith that profoundly impacts the advance of God's Kingdom is the reality of God's manifest presence. According to scripture, God is continuously with His followers (see Psalm 139:7-8; Matt. 28:20; Heb. 13:5). Yet while this God is always with us everywhere, he can manifest (show up) in varying dimensions and degrees. This is likely what Luke was alluding to when he described a fruitful season of healing in Jesus' ministry by saying, "And the power of the Lord was present for him to heal the sick" (Luke 5:17). The apostle Paul mentions the reason for these manifestations of God to the Corinthian Church while addressing the fact that they were misusing their spiritual gifts: "Now to each one the manifestation of the Spirit is given for the *common good*" (1 Cor. 12:7). When God manifests himself, he is allowing his presence to be made known for the good of blessing someone's life and revealing his Kingdom on earth.

An environment where God's powerful presence is 'showing up' becomes extraordinarily conducive to the miraculous. A good example of this is recorded in Acts 19:11-12 where Luke writes, "God did extraordinary miracles through Paul, so that even handkerchiefs and aprons that had touched him were taken to the sick, and their illnesses were cured and the evil spirits left them." Such miracles can serve as "signs that make you wonder" about God and the Kingdom that is now among us. While we prayerfully hope for such extraordinary occasions of God's manifest presence, disciples of Jesus Christ are called to pray for the sick in and out of such precious seasons of

Kingdom breakthrough. And what church would complain about having a testimony of consistent "ordinary" miracles of healing!

Humble, Dependent Prayer

Humility says, "I have a need. Please pray for me." Compassion says, "I care about your need, and yes, I will pray for you." When humility and compassion meet in this way, an atmosphere conducive to a move of God is created. James makes this point in his practical instruction on prayer:

> Is any one of you sick? He should call the elders of the church to pray over him and anoint him with oil in the name of the Lord. And the prayer offered in faith will make the sick person well; the Lord will raise him up. If he has sinned, he will be forgiven. Therefore confess your sins to each other and pray for each other so that you may be healed. The prayer of a righteous man is powerful and effective (James 5:14-16).

I have witnessed God's faithfulness to this promise countless times. Every weekend the church I led for two decades makes time to pray for the sick. The elders and ministry team are prepared to anoint and pray for those desiring prayer for a variety of things at every weekend gathering. It is not unusual to have several people indicate that they've been healed (or received a margin of healing) after receiving prayer. Sometimes the report comes later, since in some cases, the healing takes place progressively.

We also see a number of people healed in the context of the small group meetings that convene in homes throughout the city during the week. Here, in the environment of intimate Christian community, the home group worships, interacts with a portion of Scripture, and then prays for one another. Such ministry times often begin with the simple question, "Who needs prayer tonight?" Individuals sharing a need are encircled by their trusted friends and then prayed for. A few weeks ago, in a small group I attend, a woman was immediately healed of severe back pain after such prayer. We have found that God delights in humble prayer—whether it is a church elder, a new believer or a child who offers it.

When we pray for divine healing in simple dependence on God, we don't have to work anything up or try to get God's attention. He is predisposed to touch us with his healing grace, and no amount of showy behavior is needed. In fact, that only puts pressure on the person being prayed for and draws unnecessary attention to us. The key is remaining humbly focused on Jesus, our great Healer.

COMMON QUESTIONS REGARDING HEALING

Why isn't everyone healed who gets prayer?

Scripture indicates that there were special times when everyone in a certain gathering was healed. Luke describes one such occurrence in the early church: "Crowds gathered also from the towns around Jerusalem, bringing their sick and those tormented by evil spirits, and *all of them were healed*" (Acts 5:16, emphasis added). I've had the privilege of witnessing a move of God where everyone who received prayer was powerfully touched by the Lord—when literally each person experienced physical healing, deliverance, or a strong encounter with the Holy Spirit. During such times, I felt like taking off my shoes, for indeed, I was on holy ground! In church history, such occasions have been described as revival.

In contrast, there are times when people are prayed for and healing does not occur. Even Jesus experienced a limitation in one occasion of his ministry: "He could not do any miracles there, except lay his hands on a few sick people and heal them" (Mark 6:5). We also read about several "sick saints" in the New Testament: Trophimus (see 2 Timothy 4:19-20); Timothy (see 1 Timothy 5:23); Epaphroditus (Phil. 2:26-27); and Paul (see Galatians 4:13-14). The fact is, not everyone was healed in Jesus' day or in the early church.

Because today we live 'between the times' when the Kingdom of God has come but not yet perfectly, people are not always healed. Again, it is important to appreciate the kingdom tension described in Chapter 1, one that Derek Morphew references when he says, "All healing doctrines that proclaim an exact formula about healing occurring totally every time we pray in real faith reveal a fundamental misunderstanding of the nature of the present kingdom. They confuse the 'already' with the 'not yet'."[42]

When we are confronted with a "not yet" result in our lives, it's especially important to maintain an accurate view of God—who is always good, always loves us, and will always cause all things in our lives to work for good (cf., Romans 12:28). Such occasions serve to keep us humbly dependent and focused upon God who is worthy of our love and surrender—whether we are healed in a specific prayer encounter or have to wait till we see him face to face.

Doesn't God cause illness to help people grow spiritually?

I hear testimonies now and again from people who have grown closer to Jesus because of their poor health. In fact, I once got a letter from a woman who pointed out that she would never pray for someone in her family who had a physical disability because she could see how God was using that ailment to teach her family more about his love and faithfulness. Then she scolded me for inviting a teenage boy named Cade, who was having dozens of seizures every day, to come to our healing conference with an expectation of being healed. She definitely was a person who misunderstood the cause of illness in this world.

While I certainly agree that God "causes everything to work together for good for those who love him and are called according to his purpose" (Romans 8:28), I don't believe God *causes* everything in our lives. And if we believe that God uses sickness to teach us about

---

[42] Morphew, 186

his love and faithfulness, wouldn't being healed by him teach us even more about his love and character? And if we believe that sickness and disability come from God and are indeed a strategic way he chooses to help us grow, then perhaps it would make more sense for us to pray to get sick and have accidents more often so we could mature spiritually? Of course, I am being facetious, but the idea that God is the one who gives illness and infirmity simply has no precedent in the life of Jesus. As Richard Nathan writes:

> It is, of course, the case That God can and does use anything, including illness, to make his people holy! Indeed, God can use any consequence of the Fall, including divorce and church splits to make us holy, but such is not the norm. Indeed, we would be remiss in our practice of Christianity if we did not pray against such things and for God's purpose of holiness to be brought into our lives apart from sinful and broken situations. Far better for us to be made holy through prayer and Bible reading, fellowship, worship, and obedience to the commandments of God than through the brokenness caused by the Fall, such as illness or broken relationships.[43]

Regarding the young teenage boy I mentioned earlier, his family did come to the conference and Cade received prayer many times. We witnessed that after eight long years of suffering, Cade's seizures were completely gone. This young man is now able to drive and play sports like the rest of his teenage friends. All praise to Jesus!

Why doesn't divine healing always happen immediately?

Many of the people Jesus touched in the New Testament were healed on the spot. It's interesting that the Bible frequently records the

---

[43] Rich Nathan, *Empowered Evangelicals: Bringing Together the Best of the Evangelical and Charismatic Worlds.* (Kindle edition, Ampelon Publishing, 2009), Kindle location - 909-917.

length of time a person lived with a condition before the miracle took place (i.e., 38 years for the man by the pool in John 5; 12 years for the woman with the bleeding issue in Mark 5; 18 years for the woman with the spirit of infirmity in Luke 13). Perhaps these biblical testimonies are given to encourage us to remember that breakthrough can happen in an instant, no matter how long we've suffered (as happened when I was healed of hypoglycemia). Regardless of the duration of our illness, God can transform our situation in a moment, and today could be that day. This reality enables us to live with hope and faith.

Even though God often heals immediately, there is at least one instance where a "process" or "progressive" healing took place in scripture. Consider the progression that happened when Jesus prayed for a blind man in Mark 8:23-26:

> He took the blind man by the hand and led him outside the village. When He had spit on the man's eyes and put his hands on him, Jesus asked, "Do you see anything?" He looked up and said, "I see people; they look like trees walking around." Once more Jesus put his hands on the man's eyes. Then his eyes were opened, his sight was restored, and he saw everything clearly.

In my experience, many people with serious conditions are healed over time and after much prayer. A woman named Theresa started attending our church-plant in Massachusetts years ago. She and her husband were new Christians and came to us excited to grow in their faith. One night Theresa shared in her small group about a near fatal car accident she'd had in the past, which had left her with permanent spine and neck injuries, along with chronic neck and back pain. Her new spiritual family surrounded her with compassionate prayer, but Theresa was not healed. In fact, her condition worsened over the next few months. Though she was somewhat confused by this, Theresa continued to trust God, receiving prayer regularly for over a year. Then one day, as she was worshipping at church, I noticed Theresa was raising her hands and moving her head in a way that she hadn't done before. After I made my way to her I asked her what was happening. She told me that, as she was focusing on Jesus during worship, she felt the healing presence of God come upon her. A few of us began to pray for her, blessing what God was doing. Moments later, Theresa threw off her neck brace (which made me a little nervous because of the seriousness of her condition), and—to our amazement and delight—she began rejoicing and dancing before God, saying, "The pain is gone! The pain is gone!" Theresa's doctor later verified that indeed she had been healed. More praise to our Divine Healer!

The Lord never clarified why it took so long for Theresa to be healed. The mysteries of God truly keep us humble and dependent upon him. Isaiah prophetically spoke for God, saying, "As the heavens are higher than the earth, so are my ways higher than your ways and my thoughts than your thoughts" (Isaiah 55:9). We don't understand everything that happens (and doesn't happen) when we pray, but perhaps divine healing is sometimes progressive because there are other issues that must be addressed first—emotional, relational, or spiritual. Paul points this out in I Corinthians 11:30 when he alludes to sin causing physical sickness for the Corinthians.[44] And Jesus said that in some cases, physical and demonic conditions would require a more intense approach to prayer (see Mark 9:17-29). Today we must be open to the possibility that God will call us to a season of fasting and prayer to see the wounded healed and set free. And as always, we are to keep knocking, seeking, and asking God for the breakthrough we need, as he's told us to do (cf., Luke 11:9-13).

Does the use of medicine show a lack of faith in God's healing power?

Scripture indicates that God works through different avenues when he brings healing. Sometimes he uses divine healing; sometimes

---

[44] 1 Cor. 11:30 – "That is why many among you are weak and sick, and a number of you have fallen asleep."

he uses doctors and medicine, and many times he uses both! As Don Williams notes, we must remember that,

> God is both Creator and Redeemer. As Creator, He gives us doctors and medicine. As Redeemer, He gives us the gospel and the authority of Jesus through the power and gifts of the Spirit. They do not contradict but complement each other.[45]

This integrative mindset is why the Apostle Paul could encourage Timothy by saying, "Stop drinking only water, and use a little wine because of your stomach and your frequent illnesses" (I Timothy 5:23). John Wimber used to humorously say, "When I have a headache, I pray and take a couple of Tylenol. Then I give God thanks for whatever gets there first."

On a serious note, it is important to counsel people who believe they've been healed to continue taking their prescription medication until a physician has confirmed their healing. It's not a lack of faith, but rather an exercise in wisdom to approach healing this way. If the healing has happened and is verified, it can serve as an even more powerful testimony to others—including the medical world.

HEALING AND DISCIPLESHIP

Jesus gave his disciples authority and commanded them to heal the sick, saying, "Heal the sick, raise the dead, cleanse those who have leprosy, drive out demons. Freely you have received, freely give" (Matt. 10:8). Therefore, healing prayer is one of the non-negotiable ministries of the Church for all time, because Jesus not only empowered and instructed his disciples to heal the sick, he also commissioned them to pass this healing ministry on to others (Matthew 28:18-20).

---

[45] Don Williams, *Start Here: Kingdom Essentials for Christians* (Ventura, CA: Regal Books, 2006), 71.

Every true Christian is a disciple or student of Jesus—a follower who is unwaveringly dedicated to becoming like his or her Master. Therefore, every disciple of Jesus must be equipped to pray for the sick, not because. the sick will always be healed, but because Jesus commanded us to do so. I heard Dallas Willard once say, "A disciple of Jesus is one who is with him learning to be like him and who intends to say and do what Jesus would say and do, in the manner in which He would say and do it." Therefore, because Jesus prayed for the sick, we must do likewise.

In past years, the acrostic, WWJD, became popular in Christian circles. It was meant to arouse the question, *"What Would Jesus Do?"* in any given situation. Because the Gospels reveal the way Jesus responded to any number of events, and because the ultimate quest of discipleship is to become like Jesus in actual practice, we want our first instincts to be what Jesus would do—everywhere, everyday. And to *do* what Jesus *would do*, we need to internalize what He *did do*. Perhaps, when it comes to praying for the sick, a more appropriate question might be, *"What did Jesus do* when he met people who were suffering from sickness?"

Studying Jesus' life is essential for a balanced perspective of Kingdom living. Yes, Jesus healed the sick, and yes, we are called to pray for the sick as well. These are non-negotiables. But because the reality of divine healing can easily become a hyper-focus to those who have experienced it, the example of Jesus must always be our plumb line. He did not prioritize the healing needs of the sick above listening to and abiding under the leading of his heavenly Father. Jesus simply ministered to those around him who were in need as he followed the promptings of his Father.

> Jesus gave them this answer: "I tell you the truth, the Son can do nothing by Himself; he can do only what he sees his Father doing, because whatever the Father does the Son also does (John 5:19).

> For I did not speak of my own accord, but the Father who sent me commanded me what to say and how to say it.... So whatever I say is just what the Father has told me to say (John 12:49-50).

In the same way, every disciple of Jesus is meant to be led by the Word and the Spirit of God rather than robotically reacting to those around them. This is the example of our Master who promised that those with faith in him would do what he did, and even greater things, because he was going to the Father (see John 14:12). When our priority is being a faithful disciple of Jesus, we will allow God's Spirit to lead us into Jesus' lifestyle that is directed by God, for his glory and the advance of his Kingdom—a lifestyle that includes praying for the sick.

HOW TO MINISTER TO THE SICK

The good news for the sick is that Jesus is still healing today. The victory of the cross offers the same promise and hope that it did two thousand years ago, because Jesus is still taking up our infirmities and carrying our diseases (cf., Matthew 8:14-17). Yet now Jesus heals the sick through the agency of his Church. We have become his very hands and feet to carry out his will in the world today.

Jesus has given this ministry to all who follow him

While many churches allow their elders to anoint with oil and pray for the sick, participation in the basic ministry of healing must be extended to all. Scripture does not limit this ministry to the elders and clergy. In fact, Jesus goes so far as to say, "*Anyone* who has faith in me will do what I have been doing" (John 14:12). A child could well fit that description, as many have.

My son demonstrated this reality while we visited my parent's home in Southern California. My mom was suffering from a severe migraine, and at one point my five-year-old son, Andrew, ran through the family room announcing himself at high volume. I quickly asked him to use his quiet voice because Grammy had a headache. Andrew's face grew sad. Then he placed his hand on his Grammy's head, closed his eyes, and said, "Dear Jesus, thank you for Grammy's headache. Amen." As he ran off to continue his escapades, we laughed about the innocence and sincerity of his prayer. But moments later, my mom's headache faded, and soon it was completely gone. If God can use the simple prayer of a five-year-old, he can certainly use anyone!

John Wimber was fond of saying, "Everyone gets to play!" And he's right: the truth is that the ministry of Jesus is intended for every member of his body. The whole church needs to be unleashed to pray for the sick precisely because most opportunities for ministry will not happen within the walls of a church building. We must be ready and willing to pray for family, friends, neighbors and co-workers—those with whom we spend the vast majority of our time—right where we live. Unless our churches are equipping God's people to pray for the sick when the church is gathered and when it is not, those who need and want to receive divine healing may never experience what God intends for them. This is a dilemma that would be unthinkable to Jesus and the early church.

No magical formulas or methods

Some Christians are in search of an anointed 'method' for healing the sick. They want to know what to do so they can apply that formula in every situation. But interestingly, Jesus didn't give us a series of precise steps. In fact, as Richard Nathan said, "Indeed, the one pattern that is discernible in Jesus and the apostles' healing practices is that no pattern is discernible!"[46]

The truth is that Jesus used different 'methods' every time he ministered to the sick. He didn't seem to be as concerned with methodology (nor how the last person he touched got healed) as he

---

[46] Richard Nathan, Kindle Locations 853-854

did with the need and condition of the person standing right in front of him.[47] In that moment, it appears as if discerning what his Father was doing was his main focus (John 5:19). That being said, I have never met a person who wanted to emulate Jesus' approach to healing blind eyes by using mud mixed with saliva, yet that is exactly what Jesus did at his Father's bidding (cf., John 9:6). We are called to follow the example of Jesus, who kept his eyes and heart attuned to the leading of his Father. Then in humble dependency upon God's Word and Spirit, we, too, will see divine healings just as Jesus did.

Offering a Simple Prayer

Jesus is the healer, and our job in the partnership is simply to discern what the Father is doing in that moment and invite the Holy Spirit to manifest his healing power. This approach is designed to be an organic, relational one that comes as we work in tandem with God's Spirit. Our participation with God in divine healing may often be lived out through intercessory prayer. Here we ask God to touch the wounded with his healing power (see Acts 4:30). At other times, we may be led to stand humbly in Jesus' name, and with his authority command the ailment to cease and healing to come. This is the predominant approach to healing in the New Testament, both by Jesus and the early church. In both scenarios, it is God alone who heals. It just a difference in how God may desire to use us as his instruments of healing. I have found it helpful to employ both approaches in praying for the sick.

At the churches I have led, we consistently announce during worship that those who want prayer for divine healing can move at that time toward various stations on either side of the worship center. Someone from our ministry team—who has been trained to pray for the sick—is waiting at these stations to greet and pray for the person. People are also invited to receive prayer after the services. Seldom does

---

[47] Cf., Matt. 8:14-15; Luke 5:13; Luke 5:22-25; Matt. 14:34-36; Mark 7:33-35; John 9:6,7; Luke 6:10.

a week go by without a testimony of someone who has been touched and healed by God. And I really get excited about the testimonies of those who have received prayer outside the church walls! This is a tangible way God shows up and brings his Kingdom to the brokenness in our neighborhoods, schools, businesses, and hospitals. Even Costco seems to be a place where God enjoys touching people in our city! By decentralizing the healing ministry of the church, everybody 'gets to play'—wherever they are every day!

Unleashing God's people into Kingdom service will include intentional and ongoing effort by church leadership to train and encourage their congregations in healing prayer ministry—both inside and outside the church. Providing consistent opportunities for people to become equipped requires time, energy, and resources for training. But all the effort is worth it, because this is ultimately about making more and better disciples of Jesus—which is every believer's Kingdom assignment.

If you have not yet begun to pray for the sick or equip others to do so, here are some simple suggestions that may help you get started in this ministry:

1. *Encourage people to proceed with humble, expectant prayer.* As leaders, we need to nurture dependence on God as we bless and release our people to pray for the sick. When we create opportunities for them to be trained to pray during our local church gatherings, then encourage them to take what they've learned to the ailing outside the church, they will ultimately be empowered to do just that.

2. *Pray with a partner.* Jesus sent his disciples out two by two for a reason. Ministering in teams provides the needed support, encouragement and accountability to help us continually grow and persevere in this ministry. We not only learn from each other as the Kingdom is advanced, but ministering as a team also provides an ideal context for novices to apprentice with someone more experienced.

3. *Interview the person asking for prayer.* Here we ask the person who is needing prayer the simple question, "How would you like us to pray for you?" or, "Where does it hurt?" or, "What would you like Jesus to do for you today?" It's important not to hurry this interaction; you are already ministering just by listening to the person's story. Let the "pray-ee" know that you are really listening, and that you care about them, as well as their condition, by keeping appropriate eye contact while they are sharing. Be careful not to rush the interview, yet don't chat so long that you limit your actual prayer time. As you discover what the person needs, continue to keep one ear turned toward them and the other ear tuned to heaven.

4. *As the person talks, seek to discern what may be the underlying cause of their condition.* At times, it will be important to allow the Holy Spirit to show you anything that might be significant for a complete, sustained healing. Then, as you are led, ask if the pain came from an accident, or began about the same time as any other significant event in their lives. Listen for other underlining issues, such as any patterns of unforgiveness that may be hindering their healing, especially if they have received prayer many times in the past (more is said about the healing of inner wounds in the next chapter).

5. *Then pray.* After carefully listening to the person and humbly seeking to discern what God wants to do, it's time to pray. Just bring their situation to God, asking him to work in the person's life as the condition requires. Ask the Holy Spirit to come and release his healing power into the area needing his touch. Continually seek to discern how God would have you pray, and humbly follow his promptings. Note: if you sense God leading you to pray for other things as well, be sure you still pray for their specific request!

6. *Check in with the person after a few minutes of prayer.* It is often good to ask simple questions, such as, "How are you doing?" or "Do you feel any improvement yet?" or even, "Are you better, worse, or the same?" Such questions can serve to encourage or redirect the prayer focus as needed throughout your time of prayer. Pray again as the situation warrants and the Spirit leads.

7. *Offer post-prayer counsel and care.* After the prayer time is over, it is important to find out what happened (or did not happen) as you prayed. Allow for an honest appraisal of what the pray-ee feels God may have done, if anything, during the prayer session. People sometimes shy away from this sort of follow up, which is unfortunate because you may miss out on hearing a healing testimony or on discovering what else God is currently doing in their life. Plus, if there was a margin of healing, it may be wise to pray further and see what God might continue to do.[48] As mentioned before, many people experience a complete healing only after several occasions of prayer. Therefore, checking in, then praying again, then checking in again, may be helpful. And lastly, if there is no healing experienced, it is critical to encourage the person to continue trusting God and allowing others to pray for him or her. While it's difficult to hear them say, "Nothing happened," we must overcome our timidity so that we can help the person know how to respond in the moment. As you conclude, always bless the person and thank them for allowing you to pray for them.

8. *Encourage the pray-ee to remain open to God if he or she received a partial healing.* Many people experience some healing during prayer, but often additional healing occurs *after* the actual

---

[48] The common cause for avoiding the check-in and post-prayer questions is fear—the fear that "nothing" happened. Allowing such fear to sabotage the follow up is detrimental to a fruitful healing prayer ministry.

ministry time—as has already been mentioned. Therefore, be sure the person leaves the ministry time feeling loved and cared for—which alone promotes healing and an openness to further ministry.

9. *Praise God when any amount of healing occurs.* When healing does take place, it's time to worship and give thanks to God—even if the relief is only incremental. If a complete healing is believed to have taken place, encourage him or her to have the condition verified by a medical doctor, if the situation warrants that.

A Simplified Summary

- **Initiate** - "May I pray for you?"

- **Clarify** - "Where does it hurt?" "What would you like Jesus to do for you?"

- **Engage** - "Let's pray!"

- **Check in** - "How are you doing?"

- **Conclude** – Post-prayer encouragement; Seal and bless what God has done.

CONCLUSION

The good news of the Kingdom includes the fact that the God who never changes is still in the business of healing the sick and setting the captives free. Praying for physical healing must remain a core component of the church, both in our experience and as a commission given to us by Jesus. There certainly is work to be done, and we will know we are gaining ground in Kingdom living when we internalize the instincts of Jesus and the early Christians to be open to praying for the sick whenever given the opportunity. May this reality be taught in our training institutions, established in our routine church gatherings, and become the norm for what it means to be a disciple of the Risen King.

CHAPTER 5

HEALING FOR THE BROKEN HEARTED

"The Lord heals the brokenhearted and
binds up their wounds."
- Psalm 147:3

Many years ago, after planting a church in New England, my wife and I felt a clear call to move to Southern California to be part of a church planting team that was reaching out to San Diego's beach culture. God had blessed our work in New England, and we had come to deeply love the people with whom we partnered. A profound unity had developed between the leadership and the body as a whole. I had the privilege of training many gifted people during this time, so that when it was time for us to leave, the torch could be passed relatively smoothly to leaders already recognized and respected. My greatest problem now was saying good-bye to the ministry and close friends whom I had grown to love.

After announcing our decision to leave the church, Jill and I stayed in the area another month. At some point during these weeks of parties, packing, and bon voyage get-togethers with friends, I became overwhelmed by the pain and thought the only way to endure this transition from New England to California was to consciously "shut down" my emotions. This coping strategy immediately gave me what I wanted: an anesthetized heart—which at the time really came in handy. I reasoned that when we got to San Diego and settled into our new ministry context, I could begin feeling again and all would be well.

Then we arrived in California. Over the first few weeks I was surprised that I wasn't struggling with the sadness of our loss. But I also noticed I wasn't feeling much happiness either. In fact, I couldn't feel much of anything! Eventually I realized I was in trouble emotionally. While it seemed relatively easy to "turn off" my painful feelings of grief as we left the northeast, I did not have the same ability to turn my feelings back on. The numbness wouldn't go away, and now I was emotionally stuck.

One evening at church, a very perceptive woman asked if she could pray for me. Shortly into the prayer time, she inquired how I was doing grieving the loss of leaving our former church community. Her question revealed the root of my problem: I hadn't let myself grieve at all. This insight gave me permission to begin the process of healing that eventually resulted in comfort and release to my broken heart. This critical experience has convinced me that there is good news for the broken hearted—giving me faith infused expectation in my ministry with others who need the Spirit to unleash healing to their broken hearts.

GOD DESIRES AND PROVIDES FOR OUR HOLISTIC HEALING

While Jesus has clearly placed comfort, healing, and inner freedom within the reach of anyone who will trust him, many Christians today remain emotionally crippled—held captive by the pain from past failures and woundings. And though they love Jesus, they are not free to follow him as they sincerely desire. But there's good news: the gospel of Jesus Christ includes the healing of past pain. "It is for freedom that Christ has set us free" (Galatians 5:1). The unfinished business of our broken past inevitably becomes an emotional encumbrance keeping us from the life that Jesus made possible. But there is good news for the brokenhearted!

In Psalm 34:18, we are told, "The Lord is close to the brokenhearted and saves those who are crushed in spirit." Though we may grow impatient with those in despair and find their condition inconvenient for us, God chooses to be close to them; he promises to heal and bind up their wounded hearts (see Psalm 147:3). The administration of this comfort and healing is yet another manifestation of the Kingdom ministry of Jesus Christ, who impeccably fulfills the prophecy spoken by Isaiah about the coming Messiah:

> The Spirit of the Sovereign Lord is on me, because the Lord has anointed me to preach good news to the poor. He has sent me to bind up the brokenhearted, to proclaim freedom for the captives and release from darkness for the prisoners, to proclaim the year of the Lord's favor and the day of vengeance of our God, to comfort all who mourn, and provide for those who grieve in Zion—to bestow on them a crown of beauty instead of ashes, the oil of gladness instead of mourning, and a garment of praise instead of a spirit of despair. They will be called oaks of righteousness, a planting of the Lord for the display of his splendor (Isaiah 61:1-3).

Today this ministry is often referred to as "inner healing", and the remedy God promises and provides often comes packaged as more of a process than a quick fix. This is described well by Brennan Manning when he writes:

> Experientially, the inner healing of the heart is seldom a sudden catharsis or an instant liberation from bitterness, anger, resentment, and hatred. More often it is a gentle growing into oneness with the Crucified who has achieved our peace through his blood on the cross. This may take considerable time because the memories are still so vivid and the hurt is still so deep. But it will happen.[49]

---

[49] Manning, *Abba's Child*, 68.

A fundamental truth is that our Creator not only made us holistically—body, soul, and spirit—but he desires to relate to all of who we are. Yet in the church today, there is a tendency to compartmentalize the spiritual, and deem the physical and emotional less significant. This belief generates a form of self-depreciation and is a modern-day expression of the ancient Gnostic heresy where nothing really matters except issues related to the 'spirit'. Gnosticism reduces our ability to invite God's Spirit to touch those aspects of our lives that are in total disarray, because we've been erroneously made to believe that as long as our "spiritual" self appears to flourish, we are living the way God intended us to live. But our Creator values every part of us, and he has made amazing provision to interact with every aspect of our nature, including our emotions. Indeed, the Lord himself is a Man of sorrows, intimately acquainted with grief (see Isaiah 53:3).

In the community of the King, all relationships, commitments, and experiences are meant to be lived with God. Dallas Willard warns us, "If we restrict our discipleship to special religious times, the majority of our waking hours will be isolated from the manifest presence of the Kingdom."[50] This tendency is dangerous and can only be undone when we as followers of the "man of sorrows" renew our minds with the truth that Jesus is sufficient, knowledgeable, relevant, and compassionate regarding every area of our life—everyday. It's no wonder that we compartmentalize our spiritual lives when we limit the nurture and grace of Jesus to only those areas that we deem 'religious'.

HOW THE TRUTH SETS US FREE

In order to be emotionally healthy, it is critical that we appreciate the truth that God loves us just the way we are right now. In fact, the person we really are is the only person God knows. He doesn't recognize us as the person we *want* to be, or the person we believe we

---

[50] Willard, *Divine Conspiracy*, 287.

"ought" to be. He sees right through our fig leaves and masks, bringing healing grace to our lives wherever and whenever we need it. Staying current with God about how we feel is, in fact, the only way we can live a life that is free from two extremes: either letting our emotions run our lives or over-controlling our feelings.

Jesus made it clear that it is his truth that will set us free,[51] which includes being honest with ourselves *and* him. As David wrote in Psalm 51:6 (NASB), "Behold, you desire truth in the innermost being." God wants us to be truthful with him, and when we deny our feelings, God's provision of grace has no 'landing strip' on which to settle down. Brennan Manning goes so far as to say, "Whatever is denied cannot be healed."[52]

Authentic spirituality is not a matter of perfection but honesty with God, others, and ourselves. It's the basis of a fruitful Kingdom life under the reign and rule of God, which can only happen in the presence of fierce truthfulness. "The Lord is near to all who call on him, to all who call on him in truth" (Psalm 145:18). It's important to realize that God brings his grace to touch us as we truly are; that is why He came! The real 'us' is often not who we *wish* we were, or even who we are *supposed* to be by other's standards. But the abundant life Jesus promised can only be ours when we are willing to expose our own "internal imposter", our presentable (though false) self.[53] Because the imposter is not who we really are, God cannot work with this false image. Thomas Merton writes, "Every one of us is shadowed by an illusory person; a false self. This is the man I want myself to be but who cannot exist, because God does not know anything about him."[54] To call upon God in truth requires that we come to him just as we are—issues and all!

As disciples of the Risen King, freedom comes as we choose to intentionally abide in God's truth. The devil—who is called the "father

---

[51] Cf., John 8:32

[52] Manning, *Abba's Child*, 40.

[53] cf., Manning, *Abba's Child*, chapter 2.

[54] As quoted by Manning in *Abba's Child*, 34.

of lies"[55]—wars against this truth in our minds, seeding our thoughts with deception. These thoughts may feel true while they in fact are not. The enemy does this to hold us captive because believing Satan's fabrications always leads to some level of dysfunction and bondage. The apostle Paul describes this battle for our minds in 2 Corinthians 10:3-5:

> For though we live in the world, we do not wage war as the world does. The weapons we fight with are not the weapons of the world. On the contrary, they have divine power to demolish strongholds. We demolish arguments and every pretension that sets itself up against the knowledge of God, and we take captive every thought to make it obedient to Christ.

What we believe about God, ourselves, and others is of utmost importance because it critically influences how we will feel and live our lives. Here are some fundamental truths that I know from my years of following Jesus and working with others that the enemy loves to distort:

- I am fully known and deeply loved by God.
- I can be completely forgiven and walk in God's freedom every day.
- I belong to God.
- God is always with me.
- My sufficiency is found in Christ.

To experience the freedom Jesus made possible, we must take each thought captive that does not align with God's truth, and immediately refocus our minds on the truth of who God is and who we are in him. We must remain anchored to who we are and Whose we are as God's beloved. We will also need supportive friends to help us discern this

---

[55] Cf., John 8:44

truth when the lies of the enemy assault us. Four simple steps can help us renew our minds when lies begin to take hold:

- *Realize* and admit that we have believed a lie.
- *Renounce* the lie by dismissing it and shutting the door to it.
- *Replace* the lie with the truth by literally speaking the truth over ourselves, allowing it to wash and renew our minds.
- *Remain* aligned with the truth as we move throughout the day.

COMMON OBSTACLES TO OUR EMOTIONAL WELL-BEING[56]

Guilt: A powerful barrier to spiritual, emotional, and relational wholeness can be the emotion of guilt. There is a difference, however, between true guilt and false guilt, and recognizing the distinction is essential for our sustained well-being. We are meant to experience *true guilt* when our sins have not been covered by the atoning work of Christ. True guilt impacts our relationship with God, and when it is present, guilty feelings become an aid to us, serving as a red flag that points us to the truth that we have sinned. Thus, true guilt can be our friend, leading us to Jesus to confess and repent. As the Scripture tells us, "He who conceals his sins does not prosper, but whoever confesses and renounces them finds mercy" (Proverbs 28:13).

False guilt, on the other hand, is experienced when we feel guilty about something for which there is no true basis of wrong. Unlike true guilt, this is a form of neurotic guilt that does not dissipate even when we sincerely confess it to God (because there is no actual sin needing

---

[56] Some of the material in the following sections regarding guilt, anger and depression was inspired from my Doctor of Ministry class with Dr. Archibald Hart called, *Minister's Personal Growth* at Fuller Theological Seminary in Pasadena, California.

his forgiveness). For example, we may feel guilty about something for which we've already sincerely confessed, or we may feel guilty because others disapprove of our lifestyle—even though we are not violating God's Word. Surely some with a religious spirit try to control others by making them feel guilty, which is what happened when the Pharisees disapproved of the people Jesus was spending time with, or when they criticized him for healing on the Sabbath (see Matt. 21, Mark 2, 3). False guilt is something we must learn to quickly discern lest we continue to live under the influence of neurotic guilt and shame.

While *true guilt* is dealt with through humble confession and repentance *before* God, *false guilt* must be overcome by a truth encounter with God. Any thoughts and feelings that are not based on truth must be acknowledged as false, renounced, and then replaced with the truth. As the apostle Paul wrote, "We take captive every thought to make it obedient to Christ" (2 Corinthians 10:5). The apostle offers a healthy theology for dealing with false guilt when he writes:

> I care very little if I am judged by you or by any human court; indeed, I do not even judge myself. My conscience is clear, but that does not make me innocent. It is the Lord who judges me. (1 Corinthians 4:3-4)

Paul states that we are not guilty because of other people's judgments. Neither do our own judgments make us guilty before God. Each of these can lead to neurotic guilt and shame, but true guilt can only be established by God. God's judgment alone determines our guilt or innocence. His Word and his Holy Spirit reveal the truth and bring conviction of sin, which will include a healthy correspondence between our feelings of guilt and the actual state of our guilt. We can, however, neglect the convicting nudges of the Holy Spirit, which are intended to lead us to repentance. When this happens, we can develop a hardened heart, and our capacity to feel true guilt is hampered—even when we displease or grieve God. The apostle Paul warns us that in such cases, we can develop a "seared conscience", causing God to eventually give the persistent, unrepentant sinner over to a "depraved mind".[57]

The good news is that the Gospel of Jesus Christ includes powerful provision for the alleviation of all true guilt! While Christians can be thankful for feeling guilty to the extent that it indicates actual sin, when we sincerely confess and repent we will begin to habitually experience God's uncompromising forgiveness and cleansing. That is what the gospel promises and provides: "If we confess our sins, he is faithful and just to forgive us our sins and purify us from all unrighteousness" (1 John 1:9). As the great hymn proclaims:

What can wash away my sin? Nothing but the blood of Jesus.
What can make me whole again? Nothing but the blood of Jesus.
Oh, precious is the flow, that makes me white as snow.
No other fount I know, nothing but the blood of Jesus.[58]

Anger: Anger is an emotion felt when we witness or experience a perceived injustice or wounding. Feelings of anger are normal, healthy, and even helpful when they do not convert into vengeful reactions. Anger can help us rise up and take action when needed. The problem arises when anger moves from serving as a stimulus for appropriate action, to becoming an emotion that destructively targets oneself or others. Paul writes in Ephesians 4:26-27, "In your anger do not sin. Do not let the sun go down while you are still angry, and do not give the devil a foothold."

Some significant truths are revealed in this passage about anger. First, we see that being angry is not directly equated with sin. The difference between healthy anger and destructive anger has everything to do with what we do with the emotion. When hurt turns to anger, and anger becomes bitterness, and bitterness develops into some form of toxic vengeance, this results in giving the devil a foothold. And so, the apostle's exhortation to deal with anger daily is imperative for the

---

[57] Cf., 1 Timothy 4:1-2; Romans 1:18-32
[58] From the classic Christian hymn, *Nothing But The Blood* by Robert Lowry (Public Domain).

sake of one's emotional, spiritual, and relational well-being. While anger in and of itself is not wrong or sinful, the Bible strongly encourages the believer to deal with this powerful emotion quickly so that it does not turn into sin that precipitates bondage.[59]

Passive/aggressive. One unhealthy approach to coping with anger is becoming passive/aggressive. A person who regularly becomes passive/aggressive often also functions as a people pleaser. They can appear to be gentle, kind, and caring, and can even seem to handle criticism well, but in truth there is a large chasm between how he or she is actually handling anger on the inside and how he or she wants to be perceived. Someone in this condition will be passive or yielding until the anger builds-up to the point of an emotional explosion. It is not uncommon that before a big blow-up, passive aggression often gets displayed as sarcasm or little, indirect jabs and gestures. It also often results in speaking behind someone's back as opposed to the direct confrontation required in Matthew 18.

Scape-goating. Another dysfunctional attempt to resolve anger is through scape-goating. In this instance, the anger is misplaced and redirected from its true object to another who appears safer. For example, when I'm mad at my boss, I come home and kick the dog. Obviously, this scenario offers no lasting solution.

Ventilation is another approach that does not provide genuine relief from anger. Some psychologists even believe that instead of ventilation releasing us from anger and aggression, it actually reinforces and even increases anger.[60] Jesus offers a far better solution than the proverbial "blowing off steam."

Forgiveness. The only true and effective means of alleviating the negative aspects of anger comes through forgiveness. When I have been hurt in some way by another person, I often feel I have a "right"

---

[59] For example, see Psalm 73:21,22; Eph. 4:26-28
[60] cf., Archibald D. Hart, *Unlocking the Mystery of Your Emotions* (Dallas,TX: Word Publishing, 1989), 70-72.

to be angry, but the Gospel calls me to give up that right for the sake of holiness, wholeness, and healthy relationships. By forgiving, I'm in no way changing the reality of the wrong that was done to me. Rather, I am surrendering my right to live in reaction to that wrong.

To be clear, true forgiveness is a supernatural work of God, and the grace we need to forgive those who have severely wounded us essentially comes from the Lord. Thankfully, he gladly empowers us to do what we cannot do for ourselves. With a similar thought, Manning writes:

> The exigencies of forgiveness are simply beyond the capacity of ungraced human will. Only reckless confidence in a Source greater than ourselves can empower us to forgive the wounds inflicted by others.[61]

How to forgive: There are several facets included in the process of real forgiveness, or what Jesus calls "forgiveness from the heart" (Matt. 18:35):

1) First, we must honestly acknowledge that we have been hurt, and how we have been hurt. This must be followed by grieving the loss experienced in the wounding. Warning! This can be painful, ugly, and very difficult. Yet we must allow this demanding step to be the beginning of our healing process. If we don't do this, what is inside remains there—keeping us in bondage to the past.

2) Next, it's essential to confess any sinful or dysfunctional reactions we've had to the wrongs experienced. We never minimize the damage done to us, but we must take responsibility for our own sinful and dysfunctional reactions to those wrongs, asking the Lord to forgive us as we repent for the ways we may have taken matters into our

---

[61] Manning, *Abba's Child,* 68.

own hands rather than leaving them in the hands of the Lord who always judges justly.

3) Without rushing the forgiveness process, the last step is to commit to forgiving the offender. This may start as a decision of the will birthed from a desire to obey the Gospel rather than because we have a positive emotion to do so. But our willingness to forgive is a fundamental ingredient, not only to our experience of the Lord's forgiveness in our lives (see Matt 6:12, 14-15), but also in causing us to become like the One who has forgiven all our debts, which we could never repay (Matt 18:21-35).

By applying the Gospel of forgiveness to our woundings, God sets us free from a life of reaction and revenge. Because we live in a fallen world full of broken people—which includes ourselves—everyone will experience relational pain of one kind or another in this life. But though we do not have a choice about living in a fallen world, we do get to choose how we'll respond to those who wound us. Just as Jesus forgives us, so we must forgive others—which opens a path to extraordinary freedom.

I have developed a simple tool to help people work through the forgiveness process. It begins by honestly admitting that we have been offended and have not fully forgiven our offender. To recognize the symptoms of unforgiveness, ask yourself these questions:

Is there a person in my life with whom I tend to…

- Continually rehearse past wrongs and wounding scenarios?
- Avoid or treat with indifference?
- Talk about negatively to others?
- Carry a secret wish that they would somehow fail or feel pain?
- Treat in a passive/aggressive way?

- Be easily offended by?

If the answer to any of these questions is "Yes", then we are likely refusing to forgive at some level. Once our unforgiveness has been exposed, it's time to plant the cross between our offender and us.

When I use this tool, I often draw a literal cross on a piece of paper, then put the name of the offender on the top left, and the name of the offended person (or my name, if I'm working through my own woundings) on the top right. I then help the offended person list the specific details of the offense. This gives them an opportunity to begin grieving the losses incurred through the wounding. I am there to pray and coach them through this painful narrative, writing down the offenses mentioned on the left side of the cross beneath the offender's name.

The offender's name	The offended person's name
Clarify the offense:	Identify any sinful/dysfunctional reactions:
• Broken trust	• Unforgiveness
• Lied against	• Bitterness
• Gossiped about	• Resentment
• slandered	• Hatred
• Abandoned	• Avoidance
• Betrayed	• Revenge
• Abused	• Criticalness
• Etc.	• Gossip
	• Keeping a record of wrongs

As this process continues, the offended person (and I) are listening for any sinful or dysfunctional reactions to the wrongs done to them. These responses are listed beneath the wounded person's name on the right side of the cross.

After the offense(s) have been clarified and grieved, along with noting any sinful/dysfunctional reactions, it's often best to start by having the wounded person confess aloud to God his or her reactionary sins and dysfunctional behavior. Though wounded by another, taking responsibility for our own sinful reactions to the wrongs done to us allows us to experience more of the freedom that Jesus has made possible. Confessing our own offenses to God also helps build momentum toward gaining wholeness before doing the often more painful work of forgiving another's offenses against us.

Once a healthy momentum is in place, we then turn our attention toward the wounder and forgive every offense. This does not need to be rushed. In fact, it is a common mistake to move too quickly into articulating forgiveness in this process. An offended person needs to have ample time to feel the pain of the offense and grieve each aspect of the wounding scenario. And it is so important that the person is aware of the Lord's presence as they do this, inviting Jesus into every aspect of the injury.

It's often helpful to provide some vocabulary to help the wounded person verbalize forgiveness toward their offender. For example:

- "_____, I forgive you for _____."
   (Name)   (how they hurt/offended you)

- "_____, I choose this day to no longer live in reaction to what you have said and/or done against me."

- "_____, I release you from the prison of my unforgiveness."

- "Even as I have been forgiven, so also in Jesus' name I forgive you."

After forgiveness has been extended, it's important to dismiss any demonic oppression—since once the cross is applied, the enemy's right to harass us is broken. Finally, by faith and in obedience to God's Word, the wounded person should proceed to bless the offender (see Romans 12:14 and Matthew 5:43-48). Doing this is often exceedingly difficult but is the righteous and right thing to do according to Jesus (cf., Luke 6:28). I have heard numerous people testify that this culminating act of obedience played an important role in setting them free from living in toxic reaction to their offender.

Depending on the amount and level of injury incurred, forgiveness toward an offender can be an ongoing process that must be revisited again and again. We may need to return to this forgiveness tool many times to experience a sustained release from the offense, but it will come! Again, inner healing is very often not a "one stop shop," but rather a spiritual exercise of faith dealing with one layer of brokenness at a time.

It's important to say that going to the offender to confront him or her is not always a necessary step in the forgiveness process. Sometimes that becomes a way to strike back, reopening old wounds and keeping the hurt alive. The forgiveness process is primarily Godward. Discussing the offenses with the offender will often need to be pursued much later after a tangible measure healing has taken place, if at all. Employing the advice of a trusted and wise friend or counselor can be very important at this point.

Depression: Dr. Archibald Hart describes depression as, "The common cold of the emotions."[62] Yet many people hold a simplistic view of depression, thinking that depression is simply "wrong," and

---

[62] Archibald D. Hart, *Dark Clouds, Silver Linings* (Colorado Springs, CO: Focus on the Family Publications, 1993), 1.

certainly is not something that a "real Christian" would ever need to deal with. This naïve notion has caused a number of believers to be dishonest with themselves and others about their condition. Yet when we spend our energy to hide our depression behind a wall of embarrasment and shame, healing has little chance to occur. There are two major categories of depression: reactionary and bio-chemical.

Reactionary depression. Reactionary depression occurs when one has suffered emotional pain from the various losses of life. Life is full of losses, both minor and major. The loss of a loved one, an undesired change in career, a broken friendship, a failure on a test, or the first scratch on our new car, can all be losses that precipitate a state of depression. The actual cause of the depression is not really the experience of the loss itself, but rather the degree of attachment to the perceived loss. This explains why two people can experience the same incident but may have two very different emotional reactions. The degree of reactive depression can sometimes be measured by the degree of attachment that was present before the loss took place.

The path to healing for reactive depression includes discovering the losses and attachments that are causing the depression, then grieving those losses. Only mourning our losses will make space for God's healing comfort to come in. As Jesus said, "Blessed are those who mourn, for they shall be comforted" (Matthew 5:4). Mourning does not describe the state of our sadness, but rather the process of getting it "up and out". When depression comes because of a loss, we must share our hurts with God. Often a sensitive friend or a counselor can also help us grieve and mourn in a healthy way by encouraging us to share our story of experiencing a specific loss. And as we mourn our losses by shedding our tears and getting our painful narrative up and out, we create space to be filled with the healing comfort of God.

Bio-chemical depression. The second major form of depression is bio-chemical. The functions of the brain, such as thinking, memory, and feeling, are all dependent upon the healthy electrochemical transmission of signals along our nerve cell fibers.[63] When the neuro-transmitters fail to travel and connect properly with the neuro-receptors in our brain, there will be some kind of negative emotional reaction. Therapy in this case may include a combination of counseling and medical treatment.

Though positive results are common when medication is prescribed for bio-chemical depression, there is frequently a great deal of resistance associated with the use of medicine to treat depression in the body of Christ. This opposition is often due to ignorance and/or a religious spirit, which I found out first hand when I was suffering from bio-chemical depression during a problematic season of life. In a therapy session, I was informed that I was experiencing a clinical depression, and evidently, I had been enduring this depression for some time without realizing it. The therapist encouraged me to see a medical doctor to get medicine to help treat the problem. But as I left her office, I remember driving away feeling a mixture of both hope and shame.

After talking and praying with my wife, I did see a physician who recommended medication. Yet in the midst of that dark season, I received a call from a denominational leader telling me I just needed to trust God and rejoice more in the Lord. Rather than feeling his comfort, I felt his condemnation. (I'm glad it's not possible to punch someone in the nose over the phone!) Thankfully, the medication helped my neurological system readjust, providing the emotional balance I had sorely lacked. It was like putting on a pair of glasses and seeing clearly for the first time in months. Yet while none of us would choose to live with impaired vision, we attach a negative connotation to the medication that can help us see the world more clearly.[64] The

---

[63] Cf., Gerald G. May, M.D. *Care of Mind, Care of Spirit* (San Francisco: Harper & Row, 1982), 22,23.
[64] It's interesting that those who feel strongly that Christians should not use antidepressents for depression often wear prescription eyeware without a second thought! What really is the difference? In either case, seeing more clearly feels like a magnificent gift.

medication not only gave me a more accurate perspective, but I was able to deal more effectively with the situation and emotions surrounding me. In time, I was able to slowly suspend the medication as God graciously brought healing and emotional stability. And today I am grateful to God for prescription glasses…and antidepressants!

Post-adrenalin fatigue. Another type of biochemical depression is related to our adrenal system. People who live highly stressful lives are especially vulnerable to this condition. The adrenal gland is an amazing gift God has placed in our bodies to enable us to confront extraordinary situations that require a "fight or flight" response. When our ancestors encountered a saber-toothed tiger, their adrenal systems would secrete adrenalin into the blood stream, enabling them to run faster, have uncommon strength, and experience an unusual capacity to withstand pain. Adrenalin is a gift from God intended to help us ramp up physically and psychologically for an intense situation.

However, we can abuse the gift of our adrenal system when we call on it to keep going too long too often, allowing high-stress circumstances to become the norm. God has provided adrenalin for those occasional times in our lives when we need to be ready to face an abnormally strenuous situation. But when the occasional emergency becomes our constant pattern, the piper eventually comes to be paid. A depleted adrenal system leads to debilitating exhaustion and some level of depression.

Not only is our adrenal system in charge of releasing the energy we need to survive a demanding situation, it also stimulates the reward or pleasure center of the brain. Therefore, adrenalin can become addictive. Negative withdrawals take place when the pressure is finally off and the body and emotions begin to let down. But to avoid the inevitable discomfort of withdrawal, the adrenalin junkie will often turn to caffeine or some other activity or stimulant to rev him or herself back up. But the healthy thing to do is slow down, rest, and give one's body time to recover.

I've certainly encountered adrenalin fatigue while serving as a pastor over the years. After working hard all week, then spending 110% of my energy to prepare and deliver several sermons on Sunday, plus minister to those needing prayer, my Mondays were often met with exhaustion, irritability, and an emotional dark cloud. Many ministers refer to this as the "Monday blues." And if I ever had a bad headache, it was almost always on a Monday. Several years ago, Dr. Archibald Hart gave me some wisdom that has radically shifted how I deal with post-_adrenalin_fatigue syndrome. The shifts are simple: proper pacing, rest, and recovery, but observing them has resulted in my rarely experiencing the "Monday blues." Living at a healthier pace, for example, required that I prepare sermons early in the week to avoid the stress of last-minute preparation—along with the need for excessive caffeine to keep me energized in that crunch. Regarding rest and recovery, learning to schedule "down time" in my calendar after a high-energy output—like a conference or international trip—helps me recharge afterward.

Lessons from the dark night. While I would never wish a painful season of depression on anyone, such periods can become a unique opportunity for growth. During my "dark night", I learned many lessons that I may not have gained apart from this period of darkness.[65] First of all, I realized that I am not in control of my life like I thought I was. When my depression hit, I tried everything I knew to restore the "joy of my salvation," but nothing seemed to work. God exposed my pride and need for control. At times I felt like God had abandoned me, but gradually I learned that God was with me even when I could not feel or discern his presence. I also began to enjoy the smaller, slower, quieter things of life. During the dark night, I discovered a side of God and life that I would never have appreciated in the brighter seasons. I

---

[65] Helpful insights for understanding and dealing with such seasons of darkness are included in an excellent book by Brennan Manning called, *The Signature of Jesus* (Sisters, OR: Multnomah Books, 1996). See especially Chapter 7 called "Celebrate the Darkness." Also helpful is a chapter in a book by Terry Wardle, entitled, *Draw Close To The Fire* (Grand Rapids, MI: Chosen Books, 1998). The first chapter is entitled, "God Is Within The Darkness," 13-32.

can now more honestly testify of my Lord, "You are good, and all that you do is good" (Psalm 119:68). God's purpose in pruning is broader than punitive discipline. It is the fruitful branch in John 15 that is cut back in the Father's wisdom and love so that more fruit will be produced.

When difficult and confusing seasons happen, depression can be inevitable. My wife and I lived in New England for seven years, and there we learned that in winter, though our trees may have looked dead, their lifelessness was an essential part of the tree's development. This season of barrenness was necessary to cause the sap to go inward as the roots deepened. Relating this to the healing process, Terry Wardle writes:

> 'Winter' for the Christian is that time when the Holy Spirit exposes our wounds, broken places, and unfruitful habits. It is far from pleasant, and even less so if we try to hide or resist his work.[66]

Though I feel like a slow learner, I am growing to appreciate—and even embrace—these winter seasons of life that I once resisted. And thankfully, seasons do change.

Fear. Fear is a common problem most people experience, some more often and intensely than others. The Bible indicates God's knowledge of our vulnerability to fear and encourages us to "fear not".[67] To live under the grip of fear is to live in bondage, but the good news is that Jesus has put freedom from fear within our reach!

One of the difficulties in overcoming fear is recognizing what it actually looks like in our lives, since there are many faces of fear. For example, *passivity* as well as *aggression* can both be symptoms of fear. When approaching an abused dog, it may cower *or* attack. Either

---

[66] Terry Wardle, *Draw Close To The Fire*, 127.
[67] For example, see, Proverbs 3:25; Isaiah 54:4; Lamentations 3:57; Haggai 2:5; Matthew 10:31; 1 Peter 3:14

response can be provoked by the dog's fear. Imagine the futility of trying to help the dog overcome his cowering *or* attacking tendencies without recognizing the root issue. Obviously, this principle holds true for people as well.

Other common symptoms of fear include excessive busyness, procrastination, avoidance, being hyper-vigilant, clingy, walled-off, over or under confident, excessively helpful or unavailable, speaking too many words or very few. Any of these can be the fruit of fear. Fear may at times seem to serve us well, either to motivate us to get more work done or to keep us safe. Yet the sad truth is that we are never free when we live under the tyranny of fear.

Perhaps the greatest fear for many of us is the fear of relational intimacy. Henri Nouwen speaks with great insight regarding this when he writes:

> Fear is the great enemy of intimacy. Fear makes us run away from each other or cling to each other but does not create true intimacy.... Fear makes us move away from each other to a "safe" distance, or move toward each other to a "safe" closeness, but fear does not create the space where true intimacy can exist. Fear does not create a home. It forces us to live alone or in a protective shelter but does not allow us to build an intimate home. Fear conjures either too much distance or too much closeness. Both prevent intimacy from developing.... My own experience with people whom I fear offers plenty of examples. Often I avoid them; I leave the house, move to a corner where I can remain unnoticed, or express myself in flat, noncommittal sentences. Sometimes I create a false closeness with them. I talk too long with them, laugh too loudly at their jokes, or agree too soon with their opinions. Whether I create too much distance or too much

closeness, I always sense a lack of inner freedom and a resentment toward the power they have over me.[68]

The problem of fear necessitates an indirect approach to finding freedom. The apostle John alludes to this:

> And so we know and rely on the love God has for us. God is love. Whoever lives in love lives in God, and God in him.... There is no fear in love. *But perfect love drives out fear*, because fear has to do with punishment. The one who fears is not made perfect in love. (1 John 4:16,18, emphasis added)

What we learn from this text is that what we might call a "fear problem" could better be described as a "love deficit." To the degree that our minds and emotions are disturbed by fear, we are not functionally living under the influence of God's relentless love and favor. As Nouwen states, "The way to 'victory' is not in trying to overcome your dispiriting emotions directly, but in building a deeper sense of safety and at-homeness and a more incarnate knowledge that you are deeply loved."[69] No matter how great our fear may seem, the perfect love of God is greater still!

Contemplation. To experience God's transforming love, the believer needs to intentionally take time to contemplate God's radical, extravagant love. Scripture meditation, worship, and contemplative prayer are three disciplines that serve to enlarge our capacity to experience God's love. I have found that in the stillness and silence of my time with God, I can hear his voice that reminds me that I am his beloved, and that the Lover of My Soul lives within me. My fears begin to fade as I ponder the truth about Who it is that lives within. This is the Ever-faithful One who is our Ever-Present Help in times of

---

[68] Henri J.M. Nouwen, *Lifesigns* (New York: Image Books, 1990), 30-31.
[69] Nouwen, *The Inner Voice of Love*, (New York: Doubleday, 1996),42,43.

trouble.[70] He is greater than anything or anyone I will face in this world![71]

When I was in kindergarten, my family and I lived on an Airforce base. Down the street from our home lived an older boy (perhaps 7 years old) who I was terrified of for some reason. One day I asked my dad if we could take a walk down our street and pass in front of his house. I will never forget holding my dad's hand as we walked along. Next to my dad I felt a bit taller and stronger than I actually was. I remember just hoping that the big 7-year-old bully would come into his front yard as we passed by. I wanted to show off my huge dad and let that boy know (as I held tightly to my dad's hand) that I wasn't afraid!

In the same way, to the degree that we experientially know and live in light of our heavenly Father's love, we can face and overcome the fears that confront us. Our fears fade as we face them knowing we are God's beloved children, who can say, "Because my Dad is with me, I will not be afraid!"

Community. As with the entire spiritual journey, we are meant to face the challenges of our fears in a community of fellow Christ-followers. Members of our community are an essential means of grace to encourage us that we are dearly loved by God and belong to him. It is very important that we do not try to fix each other when we are afraid or minimize or catastrophize one another's fear. The greatest service believers can offer is to nudge each other toward the love that drives out fear. Yes, God desires to love the fear out of us through an ongoing encounter with his Spirit. Our part in this is to simply position ourselves to directly hear that inner voice of love and then receive and experience God's healing presence.

---

[70] Cf., Psalm 46:1
[71] Cf., 1 John 4:4

CONCLUSION

The Gospel of the Kingdom certainly is good news for the broken hearted. The ministry of Jesus on our behalf is completely sufficient to answer our most painful and complex needs, including the need for emotional wholeness. Ultimately, the answer lies not in any pill or process, but in a Person, Jesus Himself.

> Therefore, since we have a great high priest who has gone through the heavens, Jesus the Son of God, let us hold firmly to the faith we profess. For we do not have a high priest who is unable to sympathize with our weaknesses, but we have one who has been tempted in every way, just as we are--yet was without sin. Let us then approach the throne of grace with confidence, so that we may receive mercy and find grace to help us in our time of need (Hebrews 4:14-16).

CHAPTER 6

WELCOME TO THE WAR!

For though we live in the world, we do not wage war as the world does.
The weapons we fight with are not the weapons of the world.
On the contrary, they have divine power to demolish strongholds.

- 2 Corinthians 10:3,4

In 1986 I received a phone call from a troubled college student. The past few weeks her boyfriend had been behaving strangely, and his actions seemed to be getting worse. As a young pastor and recent seminary graduate, I was certain I could help resolve the situation; so, I arranged an appointment with the boyfriend in the chapel at Gordon College that afternoon.

When I arrived, the young man was already sitting in the back row of the chapel. We greeted one another, and then he began to share his struggle in detail. He'd been feeling like his thoughts and behaviors were coming under the influence of something other than himself. Though I believed in the reality of the spirit world and had read books on spiritual warfare, I'd never encountered anything like this, nor had I ministered deliverance before.

I felt uncomfortable and a bit in over my head, but I decided to ask him if I could pray for him anyway. As we began praying, a strange thing happened. His hands and body coiled up, and he was emitting an eerie moan. Figuring that I was dealing with a demon that was holding this young man captive, and not knowing what else to do, I spoke directly to the demon and said, "Come out in the name of Jesus!"

Since it was my first experience with a demonic confrontation like this, I felt even more uncertain when the manifestations increased to the point that the student's body became rigid. While attempting to cast the demon out, I tried quoting Scripture and following the example of Jesus as much as I knew how. But I must admit that the thought of running for help crossed my mind. Scared and perplexed, I unexpectedly felt the Spirit of God encourage me to command my fear and unbelief to leave. Once I did, the tangible presence of faith and peace enveloped me, and I realized that, as Satan was losing ground, he'd begun turning his attention on me—assaulting my mind with fear and doubt. Strengthened by the Lord, I again focused on the student with a renewed sense of authority, commanding the enemy to let go of this young man and depart.

I now know that sometimes things appear worse before a breakthrough occurs and they get better. That day, after a long and intense battle, the young man finally gave one extended exhale, and the fight was over. The evil presence left his body. He was now limp and soaking with sweat, yet the peace of God was all over him. We praised God together, and then I asked the Holy Spirit to fill him from head to toe. God enveloped this young man with such an amazing sense of joy that it was undeniable that God's Kingdom had advanced, a captive had been set free, and a rookie like me had been used of God in this thing we call deliverance ministry.

JESUS CAME TO SET US FREE!

The Bible affirms that as long as Christians live on this earth we will be engaged in spiritual conflict.[72] Yet this battle against the enemy is not our fight, it's the Lord's.[73] Every Christian can be assured that though Satan is a real foe who rages against us, he is a defeated foe, and Jesus came to earth to establish his victory over the enemy and his demons once and for all. The apostle John summarized it well when

---

[72] Cf., 2 Cor. 10:3-5; Eph. 6:12
[73] cf., 1 Sam. 17:47; 2 Chron. 20:15

he said, "The reason the Son of God appeared was to destroy the devil's work" (1John 3:8).

The good news of the gospel includes advancing the Kingdom of God by setting prisoners free from Satan's grip. The Father commissioned and anointed Jesus to do this, and, indeed, this was one of his essential roles and responsibilities. Jesus clarifies this when he read these words from Isaiah 61 in a synagogue in Nazareth:

> The Spirit of the Lord is on me, because he has anointed me to preach good news to the poor. He has sent me to proclaim *freedom for the prisoners* and recovery of sight for the blind, *to release the oppressed*, to proclaim the year of the Lord's favor (Luke 4:18,19, emphasis added).[74]

After Jesus finished reading he said, "Today this Scripture is fulfilled in your hearing" (Luke 4:21). Translation: I've come to take back the ground where Satan is having his way!

Jesus revealed his intention to defeat the enemy again when he says, "How can anyone enter a strong man's house and carry off his possessions unless he first ties up the strong man? Then he can rob his house" (Matthew 12:29). As George Eldon Ladd writes, "In metaphorical language Jesus interprets his own mission among men as an invasion of Satan's kingdom (Matt. 12:25-28) for the purpose of assaulting the Evil One, overcoming him, and despoiling him of his goods. The last-mentioned end is the deliverance of men from the power of satanic evil, which finds its most dramatic expression in the exorcism of demons."[75]

It is impossible to read the New Testament in its entirety and not recognize Jesus' confrontation with the enemy, which was a significant focus in his ministry.[76] Equally clear is how Jesus proved stronger and

---

[74] Jesus is here reading from Isaiah 61:1, 2.

[75] Ladd, *The Presence of the Future* (Grand Rapids, Michigan: Erdmann, 1974), 151-152.

[76] Ladd, *Presence*, 149, "The exorcism of demons was one of the most characteristic activities of Jesus' ministry."

wiser in every contest. The challenge for us today lies in discovering how his victory can become ours amid the spiritual battles we face.

THE FOUNDATION FOR VICTORY IN SPIRITUAL WARFARE

The Triumph Gained through Christ's Cross and Resurrection

The cross and the resurrection of Jesus Christ provided the fatal blow for Satan. This is where the victory was eternally won over Satan, sin (and its fruit), and even death itself. The apostle Paul declares this critical truth:

> He forgave us all our sins, having canceled the written code, with its regulations, that was against us and that stood opposed to us; he took it away, nailing it to the cross. And having disarmed the powers and authorities, he made a public spectacle of them, *triumphing over them by the cross* (Colossians 2:13-15, emphasis added).

Here Paul announces that the cross not only provided the basis for freedom from the *guilt* of sin; they also gave us freedom from the *power* of sin and its author. Jesus disarmed the enemy and his minions when he triumphed at the cross, and when anything is disarmed, its ability to have an effect is severely limited. As the writer to the Hebrews says, Jesus took on our humanity, "that by his death he might destroy him who holds the power of death, that is, the devil" (Hebrews 2:14). In describing this power we have as believers, Paul reveals our superior position this way:

> That power is like the working of his mighty strength, which he exerted in Christ when he raised him from the dead and seated him at his right hand in the heavenly realms, *far above all rule and authority, power and dominion, and every title that can be given,* not only in the

present age but also in the one to come (Eph. 1:19-21, emphasis added).

The resurrection not only raised Jesus from the dead, it also exalted him as the eternal Champion, *far above* every evil influence, including the dark powers of Satan. As we walk in obedience with Jesus, we can have absolute assurance that our Master, Jesus, is the Triumphant King (see Col 2:15)—having already defeated Satan and his demons. "The war continues, but every battle is a relatively minor skirmish in comparison to the battle won through Christ's death and resurrection."[77] What a difference it makes to face our foe under the shadow of the Almighty!

The Kingdom Come

Advancing the Kingdom on earth and Spiritual warfare fundamentally go hand in hand. Spiritual warfare could most simply be described as the collision of two kingdoms—the Kingdom of God versus the kingdom of darkness. Every advance of the Kingdom of God means that there has been a displacement of the kingdom of darkness. Quoting Susan Garrett, Clinton Arnold writes, "As the Kingdom of Satan diminishes, the Kingdom of God grows proportionately...Every healing, exorcism, or raising from the dead is a loss for Satan and a gain for God."[78] Such things do not occur without conflict. This collision of the two kingdoms is what spiritual warfare is all about. And while this conflict is not intended to be the center of our attention, we must know how to recognize, face and overcome it if we are going to be effective disciples of the Risen King.

Regarding this relationship between spiritual warfare and the Kingdom of God, theologian George Eldon Ladd states, "It is indeed impossible to interpret the New Testament teaching about the

---

[77] Clinton E. Arnold. *Powers of Darkness* (Downers Grove, Illinois: I.V.P., 1992), 123.
[78] Arnold, *Powers of Darkness*, 80, quoting Susan R. Garrett, *The Demise of the Devil* (1989), 6.

Kingdom of God except against the background of a great spiritual struggle."[79] Ladd further clarifies this when he writes:

> This background of satanic evil provides the cosmic background for the mission of Jesus and his proclamation of the Kingdom of God...Our purpose is primarily to show that the theology of the Kingdom of God is essentially one of conflict and conquest over the kingdom of Satan.[80]

As has been stated earlier, even though the Kingdom of God was powerfully inaugurated at Christ's first coming, it will not be fully manifest until he returns again. And because the Church lives "between the times," we must anticipate Kingdom breakthroughs as well as adversity and occasional setbacks. Until the Second Coming, all true soldiers of Christ will experience the uncomfortable rhythm of battles that lead to breakthroughs, then breakthroughs precipitating further battles. Yet the victories we experience now serve as tangible foretastes of the total, final triumph Jesus will execute over Satan and his kingdom when he returns.

The Power of the Holy Spirit

Warfare of any kind entails the collision of two or more powers. In the New Testament, one of the titles given to the spiritual workers of evil is "powers".[81] To achieve victory in spiritual conflict, we need a greater power than the enemy's. Thankfully, this superior power is provided to every believer every day by the Holy Spirit. As Jesus told the first generation of Christians, "You will receive power when the Holy Spirit comes upon you" (Acts 1:8). Here the word in Greek is "dunamis", from which we get our word, dynamite. Such supernatural power is mandatory for winning every clash with the enemy—good doctrine is not enough. Satan is not intimidated by our theological

---

[79] Ladd, *Presence*, 155
[80] Ladd, *A Theology of the New Testament* (Grand Rapids, Michigan: Eerdmans, 1974), 51.
[81] cf., Rom. 8:38; Eph. 6:12; Col. 1:16; 2:15.

knowledge, but he has no defense against the manifest presence and power of God because the Kingdom of God is not a matter of "talk but of power" (see I Cor. 4:20)!

The Holy Spirit is God's presence and power for the advancing of his Kingdom on earth. The incarnate Christ was dependent himself on the Holy Spirit's power in his ministry,[82] and as Jesus aligned with the Spirit's authority and power, people were amazed, healed, delivered, and transformed. This distinguished Jesus from every other religious leader of his day.[83]

> The novelty in Jesus' teaching did not consist in its form or content but in its power. He spoke, and things happened. He commanded as one who was master of demons, and they obeyed his word.[84]

Ministering in the anointing of God's Spirit is not an option for the disciple of Christ—who will undoubtedly encounter spiritual warfare. The demonic realm is supernatural, and it cannot be ousted with carnal weaponry. The apostle Paul makes this clear when he writes:

> For though we live in the world, we do not wage war as the world does. The weapons we fight with are not the weapons of the world. On the contrary, they have divine power to demolish strongholds (2 Corinthians 10:3-4).

The church today desperately needs to understand and utilize the power Jesus has given us.[85] A.W. Tozer noted that the enemy is certainly aware of this power source, and we must be as well:

---

[82] cf., Luke 5:17, "And the power of the Lord was present for him to heal the sick."

[83] cf., Matt. 7:29; Mark 1:21-28; Luke 4:36,37

[84] Ladd, *Presence*, 166.

[85] Concerning the churches need for supernatural power, A.B. Simpson, *The Holy Spirit - Volume 2* (Harrisburg, Pennsylvania: Christian Publications, Inc., 1896), 84 writes, "We cannot leave out any part of the Gospel without weakening all the rest; and if there ever was an age when the world needed the witness of God's supernatural working, it is this day of unbelief and Satanic power."

He [Satan] opposes the doctrine of the Spirit-filled life by confusing it and surrounding it with false notions and fears. He has blocked every effort of the Church of Christ to receive from the Father her divine and blood-bought patrimony. The Church has tragically neglected this great liberating truth, that there is now for the child of God a full and wonderful and completely satisfying anointing with the Holy Ghost.[86]

It is impossible for us to be victorious in our ministries today without fully utilizing the power of God's Spirit, which Jesus depended on for success. The advance of the Kingdom in the power of the Spirit was the early church's common experience as revealed in the book of Acts and many of Paul's letters. Can we expect to succeed with less? As Don Williams writes:

Since the Devil's activities are not limited to the Apostolic Age (he is no 'dispensationalist'), we continue to need the powerful manifestation of God's authority in our age in order to overcome his works.[87]

CAN A CHRISTIAN BE DEMONIZED?

As we see God's kingdom advance, we will inevitably encounter the demonic realm, which will often appear in or around those to whom we are ministering—even in the church. Unfortunately, many have been erroneously taught that a true Christian cannot be demonized, while the truth of Scripture and Church history demonstrate otherwise. So how did this error come about?

---

[86] A.W. Tozer, *How To Be Filled With The Holy Spirit* (Camp Hill, Pennsylvania: Christian Publications Inc.), 37-38.
[87] Don Williams, *Signs, Wonders, and the Kingdom of God* (Ann Arbor, Michigan: Servant Publications, 1989), 136.

One contribution to this false idea is the fact that the Greek word "daimonizomai" is often translated, "demon possessed." But this single Greek word is better translated, "demonized" or "demon influenced." There certainly are situations under which a Christian can experience being demonically influenced. Yet, because the Spirit of God lives within all true, born-again believers, I would agree that a true Christian cannot be *possessed* by demons, but the effects of demons are real—regardless of whether they are *in*, *on*, or *around* someone.

In the New Testament only the Gerasene demoniac is described as totally controlled by evil spirits.[88] All other reports of demonization in the New Testament describe persons partially and/or occasionally bound, whether it be physical, emotional, or spiritual in nature. Yet, this partial or occasional influence can be potent and, when left to itself, devastating in its effects.

Jesus regularly delivered those who were held captive by demons, and he has commissioned his church to do the same. If demons manifested wherever Jesus went, we can bet they'll show up around us as well when we serve faithfully in his name. And those in need of Christ's freedom will include members of his body.[89] I have personally cast demons out of many people, and all them were believers! This is true in part because when I minister to a non-believer who is demonized, I first lead that person to give his or her life to Jesus; then that person is able to participate in the process of gaining spiritual freedom over the dark powers they're facing.

FOOTHOLDS FOR THE ENEMY

As we've already discussed in Chapter 5, when Christians disobey God, the devil can gain access to, or establish a foothold in their

---

88 Cf., Matt. 8:28-32; Mark 5:1-20; Luke 8:26-39
89 For a thorough study on this issue, see C. Fred Dickason, *Demon Possession and the Christian* (Westchester, Illinois: Crossway Books, 1987).

lives—especially when the sin becomes a pattern or way of life. "In your anger do not sin. Do not let the sun go down while you are still angry, and do not give the devil a *foothold*" (Ephesians 4:26-27, emphasis added). The Greek word translated "foothold" in the New International Version is the word *topos*. It can also be rendered, "place, opportunity, chance."[90] Thus, through our unconfessed sin we can give the devil a *place* in our lives, an *opportunity* to harass us, a *chance* to oppress us, an entry point for the demonic to take ground (sometimes referred to as a 'stronghold'). If we harbor unforgiveness, pride, idolatry, and unclean thoughts, Satan gains permission or the "right" to harass us, which is especially true when dabbling in the occult. Such activity allows the enemy access because the person opens the door to another kingdom. And since Satan will take any ground he's given,[91] understanding how and where he's obtained entry is critical in closing that door, especially when casting out demons.

What I have discovered is that the freedom that Jesus has made possible cannot be achieved until the demonic footholds have been exposed and removed. The ministry of deliverance progresses much faster and more easily when the enemy's right to harass has been uncovered and dealt with. It's important to clarify that strongholds and footholds are not demons but are the arenas in which demons have been given a place to access and inhabit a person's life, either through believing and embracing a lie or through willful disobedience. In spiritual warfare, we not only "demolish strongholds" (2 Corinthians 10:4), but we also "cast out demons" (Matt. 10:8).[92]

---

[90] William F. Arndt, F. Wilbur Gingrich, *A Greek-English Lexicon of the New Testament* (Chicago: The University of Chicago Press, 1957), 830, 831.

[91] Cf., Eph. 4:26-32; 2 Cor. 2:9-11; Lev. 19:31; 1 Tim. 6:9.

[92] Neil Anderson suggests that, "Freedom from spiritual conflicts and bondage is not a power encounter; it's a truth encounter" (*The Bondage Breaker*, 22). Though Anderson offers much helpful insight into dealing with the strongholds of the Enemy, this is an inadequate and misleading statement. It takes *both* truth and power to set the captives free from spiritual bondage. The "truth encounter" can deal with the strongholds, but it takes more than naked truth to cast out demons. Deliverance from demonic forces most certainly requires a "power encounter."

I have learned the hard way that freedom is not gained and sustained when I've demanded a demon to leave without taking care of the strongholds in that person's life. Once during the ministry time of a small group meeting I was leading, a young man (I will call him Peter) suddenly fell on the floor and began to shake violently. After trying to reassure the group that all was well, I knelt next to Peter and began to boldly say to the demon, "I command that you come out. You have no right to harass this young man." After several more minutes of confrontation, Peter turned and looked straight into my eyes and said with a growling voice, "Yes, we do have the right!" Instantly it became clear that Peter had "given the devil a foothold." In fact, we soon found out that he had given the devil a number of them. Sadly, we could not help Peter gain freedom that night because he refused to repent of his habitual sin. Regrettably, he left the meeting in bondage.

For someone to acquire Christ's freedom, they must turn away from any known, unconfessed sin and follow Christ's ways. By implementing this fundamental principle of deliverance, I have had much greater success in helping the demonized gain and maintain freedom. Without this act of willfully surrendering their lives to the kingdom of light, the enemy can continually harass, torment, and hold that person in bondage to the dark powers.

It's worth mentioning that, whether we suspect the presence of demons or not, it's healthy for all of us to decisively deal with sin and anything appearing to be a stronghold in our lives or the lives of those we disciple. This is a basic function of discipleship, and when we are following Christ, demonization need never be automatically assumed. In fact, I do not believe it is wise (or necessary) in most cases to tell a person when I think they have a demon (even if they do) until the Spirit exposes it. In his earthly ministry, Jesus didn't go around searching for demons. But when he entered a village, his Holy, Kingdom presence would expose the demonic when it was present. This holds true today. If there is demonization, it will reveal itself as we deal with the strongholds in a person's life. This is why I've witnessed such a strategic relationship between discipleship, inner healing, and effective deliverance.

RENOUNCING THE OCCULT AND IDOLATRY

Jesus stated that no one can serve two masters.[93] A believer must not esteem anything or anyone higher than the Lord Jesus Christ. Though I will primarily be addressing the bondage caused by participation in the occult, there are a number of other idolatrous practices that require the same treatment and cure, and the principles in this section can successfully be applied to other areas of need as well.

When it comes to the occult, some people get involved intentionally, but others step into the darkness unknowingly—unaware of what they are getting into. Many people are searching for a spiritual reality or an encounter with the supernatural, and a lot of Christians have walked through a gamut of occult practices before finding Jesus. This is what happened to the believers in the city of Ephesus:

> When this [a powerful spiritual encounter] became known to the Jews and Greeks living in Ephesus, they were all seized with fear, and the name of the Lord Jesus was held in high honor. Many of those who believed now came and openly confessed their evil deeds. A number who had practiced sorcery brought their scrolls together and burned them publicly. When they calculated the value of the scrolls, the total came to fifty thousand drachmas. In this way the word of the Lord spread widely and grew in power (Acts 19:17-20).

For Jesus' name to be held in "high honor", his power had to surpass that of the demonic realm. Experiencing that power led the

---

93 Cf, Matt. 6:24

Ephesians to turn toward Jesus and away from all that contradicted his Lordship, confessing and renouncing every idol. Many of these Ephesian believers had been involved in sorcery, which Webster defines as, "The use of power gained from the assistance or control of evil spirits." Because God created us with a hunger for his presence, people seeking a genuine encounter with the supernatural will settle for Satan's counterfeit if they don't experience the true Source. Idolatry was commonly accepted in the Ephesian culture. Our society is also heavily saturated with idolatry and the occult in many places, shapes, and forms.

When the Ephesians turned to Jesus, they took a radical stand against their idolatrous practices by openly confessing their evil deeds. This meant that they audibly and specifically admitted their sins to God in the presence of others. Public confession can be a very effective form of spiritual warfare. With every sincere confession, Satan's dominion is weakened, and Christ's reign and rule grows stronger. Notice that after Luke describes the public confession and renunciation done by the Ephesian believers, he writes, "In this way the word of the Lord spread widely and grew in power" (Acts 19:20).

Beyond their verbal confessions, the Ephesian believers also visibly burned their occult scrolls, which was another form of renunciation. To renounce means to give a decisive declaration of one's complete breakage with something linked to a specific idol. In their case, the Ephesian Christians burned their valuable scrolls, which meant an immense financial loss to them, as well as a severing of their attachment to the dark powers. This illustrates the fact that Christians must be willing to renounce even the "seeming benefits" that the occult offers. Whether it's books, drugs, paraphernalia, clothing, relationships, a job, or whatever the benefits may be; everything must be relinquished to Jesus. In fact, the devil often uses these "seeming benefits" as a cover to camouflage himself—offering something that looks promising but eventually serves to capture and shackle the victim. Then, once lured in, deception keeps that person in darkness and ever-increasing bondage.[94]

It is critical that any participation in the occult be specifically confessed as sin and renounced with a formal, once-and-for-all declaration of one's complete break with Satan and his power. Often when that happens, the "seeming benefits" will surface; they must be surrendered as well. These can be exposed by answering the questions, "Why did I involve myself in this?" or "What was I hoping to get from this that I wasn't willing to seek from God?" Those things that seem like benefits soon become traps that catch and enclose the blinded seeker.

Through the years I've heard various arguments stating that repentance and renunciation for past participation with the occult is unnecessary. I've heard some say, *"I didn't know I was in league with Satan when I did this."* But does that awareness really matter? A child may not know that they'll be burned when they place their hand in a fire, but their lack of understanding makes no difference to the flame—the fire burns them anyway. Others have said, *"I only dabbled in the occult one time",* or *"I only did it for fun".* Look at your hand after putting it into the flame one time. (Please do not really do this!) The fire doesn't care how often we expose our flesh to it—the action results in a burn. And if our motivation for playing with fire was just to have fun, then "fun" is a seeming benefit that also needs to be confessed and renounced.

In my years of ministry, I have seen that thorough repentance and renunciation are imperative when dealing with the occult. Consider the story of my friend Richard, who regularly suffered from migraine headaches. While praying for him, I sensed the Lord wanted to heal him, but his headache did not go away despite praying for some time. As we discussed his situation, Richard reported that he'd been living with these migraines for seven years. After more prayer, the Lord reminded him that seven years earlier, he'd spent time exploring the occult. He explained that he just "did it for fun," but after sharing the

---

[94] Interestingly, the word "occult" means, "hidden", and the occult is full of hidden practices.

importance of shutting those doors once and for all, Richard confessed and renounced his participation in it. Still, the headache persisted.

The next day, Richard stayed home from work due to the intensity of his headache. While lying in bed, the Lord reminded him of the occult paraphernalia he'd kept in his basement. Prompted by God, Richard went downstairs and started throwing everything away that he had kept. With his head still aching, he grabbed the last item—a record album of a witchcraft ceremony—and tried to break it. But even when he hit it against a hard surface, the vinyl did not even crack. Finally, with Richard's persistent effort, the record snapped into pieces, and at that very moment Richard's headache stopped. When he told me the story, we rejoiced together, and twenty years later he's never had another migraine. Now that's the power of the gospel!

Richard's story demonstrates the importance of repentance and renunciation, which are not merely academic exercises but engage real issues of the heart.[95] We won't see transformation take place unless we are motivated by a sincere heart; only that will bring the fruit of repentance.[96] Paul alludes to repentance and renunciation when he instructs Christians to "overcome evil with good" (Romans 12:21). Because people get involved with the counterfeit in an attempt to fill a heart void, freedom must include inner healing and having the void filled with the reigning presence of Christ once the idols are renounced. God is jealous for our hearts because it's from the heart that our love and commitments flow. And Jesus is committed to recapturing our hearts by providing the tools of repentance and renunciation.

Once we have thoroughly confessed and renounced every act of participation with the occult and applied the gospel to every known

---

[95] A simple verbalization of renunciation may not bring spiritual freedom when an additional action is also required. The believer simply needs to be humble and willing to obey any directive given by the Lord through his Word and Spirit.

[96] This point is also made in Daniel 4:27 where the following exhortation is given; "Renounce your sins by doing what is right, and your wickedness by being kind to the oppressed. It may be that then your prosperity will continue."

stronghold of the enemy, we can, with authority, command all related demonic influences to be broken and dismissed.

SETTING THE CAPTIVE FREE

If in our ministry to someone we become convinced that the person is demonized, here are some practical steps that can be helpful:

1) Remember our struggle is not against flesh and blood, but against the spiritual forces of evil in the heavenly realms (Eph. 6:12). Therefore, we must maintain a heart of compassion toward the person being held captive, realizing that Jesus came to set this person free.

2) If you are not sure the person is a born-again follower of Jesus, ask them. And if they are not, encourage them right then to put their faith in Jesus; then they can participate with God's Spirit in their own deliverance.

3) Tactfully explain what you are about to do (i.e., "Let's pray and get rid of the evil presence that's been harassing you", etc.). As you begin, assure the person that you are committed to standing with them through this process for the sake of their freedom.

4) Before you proceed with the deliverance, make sure the person understands the difference between when you will be talking to him or her, and when you will be confronting the demon(s). Francis McNutt points out the importance of this:

> Our concentration on driving out demonic forces must never overwhelm our priority of ministering Christ's healing and mercy to a wounded human being. We are not primarily ministering anger to demons, but we are ministering love to wounded people. The

persons we minister to must be able to sense that we love them.[97]

5) As you transition to the formal ministry time, begin by praising and thanking God for his victorious provision and presence. Ask for the Holy Spirit's protection, and that he would guide and guard all those involved in the session. Ask the Lord to release his authority, power, and discernment during the ministry time, since discernment is an essential ingredient in deliverance.

6) It's helpful (though not essential) to maintain eye contact with the person to whom you are ministering. The eyes can function as windows to the soul. Encourage the person to maintain eye contact with you, if possible, though sometimes, for various reasons, this is too difficult for them.

7) Before confronting the demon(s), help the person feel safe by prayerfully assisting them to be aware of the Lord's loving and powerful presence. Their feeling safe is vitally important. Then, in a normal voice, use the authoritative name of Jesus Christ to command the demon to depart without harming anyone as it goes. You can send the demon to Jesus, announcing that he will decide its fate, and demanding that it (or they) never come back.

8) All along the way, ask the Holy Spirit to fill every void that is being created as deliverance is happening.[98] Then close with a few minutes of prayer and praise, focusing on the victory and all-sufficiency of Jesus Christ, declaring his finished work on the cross and ultimate victory over all principalities and powers.

9) Lastly, ask the person what happened as you were praying. It's important to hear what they experienced and

---

[97] Francis MacNutt, *Healing* (Altamonte Springs, Florida: Creation House, 1988), 226.
[98] Cf., Luke 11:24-26; 2 Cor. 3:17

encourage them to keep walking in the light of God's truth and presence. Offer words of encouragement, loving exhortation, and appropriate counsel as needed. Then speak a prayer of blessing and protection over them and all who were involved in the deliverance session.

PERSEVERING THROUGH A DIFFICULT DELIVERANCE

Deliverance is what happens whenever the Lord breaks the enemy's influence over a person's life and sets them free. While this ministry can be demanding, it is critical to persevere, allowing the Holy Spirit to lead the way. Listening closely to him gives us the 'keys' necessary to bring freedom to each person we pray for.

The enemy often works hard to cause those ministering deliverance (as well as the person receiving ministry) to lose heart and give up before there is a solid victory. We must resist the temptation to quit, and here are some ways that can assist us as we go forward:

1) Feel free to take a break as needed. That's also a good time to stop and check in with the person about how they are doing, what they are feeling, thinking, or hearing.

2) Ask your prayer partner if they have any specific discernment that would help the process.

3) The Lord may bring Scripture to mind for you to read that applies to this particular situation. In some cases, God has prompted me to sing a worship song over the person to weaken a demonic stronghold.

4) If it seems like a long battle with little or no breakthrough, there may be a need for exploring the possibility of other strongholds. This will often require more confession, renunciation, or inner healing.

5) Sometimes it's best to arrange another appointment. Perhaps it would be helpful for the person to prayerfully do some Biblical homework before you meet again. In this

case, assure the person of Jesus' love and sovereign rule, and that his promise is to lead them into complete freedom and wholeness as they cooperate with him.

PRAYING ON THE ARMOR OF GOD

When the apostle Paul instructed Christians regarding spiritual warfare, he gave them an emphatic exhortation meant to be taken seriously.

> For our struggle is not against flesh and blood, but against the rulers, against the authorities, against the powers of this dark world and against the spiritual forces of evil in the heavenly realm. Therefore put on the full armor of God (Eph. 6:12-13).

Each of the six pieces of armor Paul mentions are strategically designed to cover areas that are vulnerable to the "devil's schemes" (v.11). In 2 Corinthians 2:11 Paul assures believers of the advantage we have because, "We are not unaware of his [Satan's] schemes," which are disclosed to us through the Word of God and by the Spirit of God. Therefore, as we put on all the spiritual armor (we cannot afford to pick and choose!), the One who knows the enemy provides everything we need to overcome the strategies of the dark powers.

It's important to note that this is the armor *of God*. God has made *his* armor available to the Christian warrior, and our responsibility is simply to put on what the Lord has provided. Through the years the Lord has taught me to put on the armor of God daily and utilize my spiritual weaponry in order to be effective in advancing God's Kingdom.

The Meaning and Purpose of the Full Armor of God

The *belt of truth* can refer to three things. First, it is a call to commit to knowing the Word of God. The Scripture is our God-breathed battle manual, and it is meant to thoroughly equip us for every good work.[99] If Jesus used the Word of God to combat the devil, we must know and use the truth of God's Word as well.[100] Secondly, the belt is a call to truthfulness. This speaks of our heart integrity, as the enemy can easily gain the advantage when there is hypocrisy. This is not referring to perfectionism, but simple honesty before God and man. And thirdly, to tighten our belt, we must exhale anything we have believed that is not God's truth, and inhale only what the Lord says, i.e., that we are totally known and loved by him, that he is always with us, and that as our All-Sufficient God he will provide all we need.

The *breastplate of righteousness* covers the life center, or heart, of the Christian. This means our "right standing" with God is a gracious gift received by faith, and, among other things, the righteousness of Christ enables redeemed mankind to minister "in Jesus' name". Unfortunately, the devil knows this all too well; therefore, he consistently seeks to accuse and condemn the saints.[101] His tactic is to get the believer to look inwardly and become fixated on his or her weaknesses and failures. This inward distraction can cause us to believe we are not worthy to stand before God as a son or daughter, much less as a minister of Christ—which quickly takes us out of the battle! Putting on the breastplate of righteousness is a call to remember that we have been made worthy by God's grace, and we must rely wholly on the fact that our "right" to minister is a gift from God, not a reward for being good.

The Christian soldier must also have his or her *feet fitted for readiness with the gospel of peace.* An effective soldier is one who is always ready for battle, remembering that the enemy doesn't take vacations. We must be prepared for the attacks that come unannounced,[102] as well as any unexpected opportunities to advance the Kingdom.[103] This spiritual

---

[99] cf., 2 Tim. 3:16,17
[100] cf., Matt 4:4, 7, 10
[101] cf., Rev. 12:10
[102] cf., I Peter 5:8
[103] cf., I Peter 3:15

mobility is gained as we walk daily in the Gospel of peace, enjoying peace with God, with others, and with ourselves. Then we will be spiritually flexible; ready to walk securely wherever the Lord takes us.

The *shield of faith* is provided to protect the soldier from the enemy's long-distance tactics. The devil would rather weaken and defeat us from a distance than face us head on. He hurls flaming missiles at us that include doubt, deception, disbelief, discouragement, accusation, fear, and temptation. These are designed to take our eyes off the Lord and what he has instructed us to do, as the victory belongs to those who "walk by faith and not by sight" (2 Corinthians 5:7). Therefore, considering this scheme, we must continually fix our eyes on Jesus and act in response to his commands—using our shield to protect us from any distracting arrows.

Paul himself defines the *helmet of salvation* as the Christian's hope.[104] Soldiers of Christ must daily rely upon the fact that they are securely saved—they belong to Jesus forever—and that nothing, not even demonic rulers, possess the power to separate them from the love of God that is in Christ Jesus our Lord (see Romans 8:38-39). Being sure about tomorrow, we are free to live courageously today, with our minds protected by the truth that we are God's children… forever!

The *sword of the Spirit* is the only offensive weapon. The soldier of Christ is reminded that the sword that overcomes the enemy is the Word of God. A verse of Martin Luther's famous hymn, *A Mighty Fortress Is Our God*, makes this point in a marvelous way:

> *And tho' this world, with Devil's filled,*
> *Should threaten to undo us;*
> *We will not fear, for God hath willed*
> *truth to triumph through us.*
> *The prince of darkness grim, we tremble not for him;*

---

[104] cf., I Thess. 5:8

His rage we can endure, for lo! his doom is sure,
One little word shall fell him.

The enemy is not threatened by our words, but only by the Word of God. While the "belt of truth" may include our commitment to gain a general knowledge of the Scripture, the "sword of the Spirit" refers to being able to apply specific Scriptural truths to a specific situation as directed by the Holy Spirit. An excellent example of this is when Jesus used the Word of God to overcome Satan in the desert by saying, "It is written: 'Man does not live on bread alone, but on every word that comes from the mouth of God.'".[105]

An Armor Prayer

It is significant to note that directly following the exhortation to "put on the full armor of God," we are told to pray, because the armor of God and the ministry of prayer go hand in hand.[106] The following is a suggested prayer that I have written for putting on the full armor of God:

> "Dear Lord, I quiet myself before You... You who are my Fortress and Peace in the midst of the battle. As I go forth today in your strength, I praise and thank you that you are in me, and you go everywhere with me, making me strong by your mighty power. Please anoint me afresh with your awesome Spirit. Thank you for your armor, which you have given me for my victory. I praise you Lord that you have provided me with what I need to stand fast against the devil's schemes. I now take up each piece and pray it on.
>
> I take up the *belt of truth* and buckle it around me. I am so thankful for the Word of God I have prayerfully read today. Please renew my mind and instruct my

---

105 cf., Matt. 4:1-11; Luke 4:1-13
106 cf., Eph. 6:18-20

heart with it for your glory. Today I will walk according to the Truth, for I know that on that path is real freedom. I will also walk in truthfulness. I now confess and repent of any hypocrisy. I will seek to live truthfully before you and others.

I put on the *breastplate of righteousness*. Once again, I rely on the fact that you have covered me with your righteousness, and I do not go forth today because I am worthy in myself. You are my righteousness, and you have made me worthy to worship and represent you by grace. I know I am your beloved, and upon me your favor graciously rests.

I now apply the Gospel of peace in order that my *feet are fitted for readiness*. I want to be ready for the unannounced attacks of the enemy, as well as the unannounced opportunities to minister in Jesus' name. Show me Lord if there are ways in which I am not at peace with you, with others, or myself. I now apply the Gospel as needed (confession, forgiveness, casting cares upon the Lord, etc.).

I take up the *shield of faith*. Lord, as I move into this day, I fix my eyes upon you. I will "walk by faith and not by sight." I will be led and influenced by you and not the flaming arrows of the enemy. When the enemy sends his missiles of doubt, discouragement, disbelief, accusation, fear, or temptation—I will hide myself in you.

I put on the *helmet of salvation*. Before I go into battle, I renew my mind in the truth that I am securely saved, that I belong to you forever, and that even demonic rulers do not possess the power "to separate me from the love of God that is in Christ Jesus my

Lord." Knowing I am eternally anchored to you, Lord, I am free to courageously obey you today.

Finally, I take up the *sword of the Spirit*, which is the Word of God. Holy Spirit, guide me today in speaking forth and applying your Truth as needed in order to advance your Kingdom and dethrone your enemy. I want to walk and minister in the light of your written and prophetic Word. Under your anointing, I will unsheathe the Sword and apply specific Scriptural truth to specific situations as you direct me by your Spirit.

I rise now and go forth in the power of your name and in the comfort of your loving presence, for your glory and fame. Amen."

CONCLUSION

We have an enemy, but he has been defeated by the cross and resurrection. As we take the territory back that rightfully belongs to the Victor, the devil and his legions may fight us, but they have already lost the war. Thus, in the name of the Risen King and in the power of his Spirit, fully clothed in his armor, we are taking back what belongs to Jesus as we partner with him to set the captives free and see his Kingdom come on earth as it is in heaven.

PART 3

THE COMMUNITY JESUS MADE POSSIBLE

CHAPTER 7

MAKING SPACE FOR GOD

A spiritual discipline is the concentrated effort to create some inner and outer space in our lives...

Through a spiritual discipline we prevent the world from filling our lives to such an extent that there is no place left to listen.[107]

After an exceptionally demanding season of ministry, I decided to take a four-day personal retreat at a nearby monastery. Worn out, frustrated, and needing God's intervention, I went with the simple objective of getting some much-needed rest, but I soon realized that God had something much more significant in mind.

After the Guestmaster showed me my room, I settled down at my desk to jot down some notes in my journal. I was surprised at the intensity behind the words I began to write: "I do not want to minister professionally again until I am delivered of this endless stress and strife, and until God is able to renew my heart with a fullness of love *from* and *for* him and others. Have mercy on me, Lord." Then I indulged myself in a needed nap.

The next morning I was eager to explore the abbey, but after several hours of "holy leisure," I became acutely aware of how uncomfortable I had become. Spending time alone in repetitive hours of solitude and silence felt monotonous, and the deafening quiet was exposing the noise inside me. In fact, my plunge into this sacred monastic routine clearly revealed how much I apparently needed

---

[107] Henri J.M. Nouwen, *Making All Things New* (New York: HarperCollins Publishers, 1981), 68.

activity and stimulation to feel good, and how much I was oriented toward performance and control. I went to take a break from what was breaking me, but I discovered that without my projects, appointments, and the demands of ministry, my sense of significance had sorely diminished. Even my identity felt somewhat at risk. I wondered, "Who am I apart from what I do?" And though these were helpful insights, they didn't bring the peace and serenity I needed and longed for.

By the fourth day, the slower, quieter, more contemplative path of the Benedictines was starting to forge an internal shift in me. I found God's peaceful presence in a measure I had never known before. God had used my time at the monastery to do a deeper, more thorough work than I'd anticipated. Simultaneously, I'd discovered the key to what would continue to inform my fruitfulness and joy in Christ and ministry—noting this in my journal:

> This afternoon I spent most of my time walking and praying and simply enjoying the beauty of the Abbey. In all my strife and hurry, I have missed so much that is good in life. Most of my focus these past four days has simply been on loving you, Lord, thanking you, and receiving your love. Lord, this has been wonderful beyond words. I want to continue the discipline of really remaining *with you* when I leave. Grace me to learn to abide in your peace through any tribulation you are pleased to bring my way.

In the decades following that retreat, the spiritual disciplines I embraced and committed to at the monastery have allowed me to position and reposition my life in God's truth and empowering presence. This gracious provision has enabled me to flourish in life and ministry, and has served to sustain me through the occasional seasons of dryness and difficulty. And I believe that the disciplines described in this chapter are an indispensable part of the life that Jesus made possible.

EMBRACING THE LIFE JESUS MADE POSSIBLE

There is a life with God that is abundant and fruitful, one that can only be lived in continuous connection with him. Such a life has been put within our reach, and this life is God's gracious gift to us. Yet it is our responsibility to consistently reach out and embrace the hand that is reaching toward us. Our response to God's invitation to live in his Kingdom must be done in continuous cooperation with his right to reign and rule in our lives. Christ's Kingdom call is not primarily a call to power, programs, or even ministry. It is not a demand that we clean up our act or try harder. It is, first and foremost, a call to God himself—our King. It is an invitation to live in continuous, willing surrender to the King's reigning presence within us, to One who truly is a "friend who sticks closer than a brother" (Proverbs 18:24). Foundational to seeing this life become a reality is our desire to carefully follow the example of Jesus—who lived faithfully and fruitfully in our very world. Becoming more like Jesus is the essence of true spiritual formation.

FOLLOWING JESUS' EXAMPLE

I'm grateful that my three children chose to wear bracelets that declared their aspiration to be like Jesus. Their visible WWJD bands served as a reminder of their intentions, as well as providing them an occasional opportunity to share with friends their love for God. Yet while many of the bracelets' owners have sincerely desired to do what Jesus would do in the face of an unannounced opportunity or temptation, they have not been equally committed to the essential (though less spectacular) elements of Jesus' private life.

If we want to live like Jesus, we must emulate all his habitual patterns. Our Lord often slipped away from the crowds to be alone with his Father. This discipline is often overlooked, but it is a key component to our Lord's fruitful life. "Following 'in his steps' cannot be equated with behaving as he did when he was 'on the spot.' To live as Christ lived is to live as he did *all* his life."[108] The Gospel writers tell us that very early in the morning while it was still dark, Jesus got up, left the house and went off to a solitary place to pray (see Mark 1:35), and that he often withdrew to a lonely place to commune with his Father (see Luke 5:16). If we want to be like Jesus, we must take his example to heart.

It's easy, even popular, to focus on the *public* aspects of Jesus' life—how he proclaimed the Kingdom, healed the sick, and demonstrated compassion to the marginalized. But rarely do many focus on Jesus' *secret* life with the Father. Yet this holds the key to our living as Jesus lived, because Jesus demonstrated that true Kingdom influence flows out of *hiddenness*. And if God the Son needed to get up before dawn to align his heart and mind with his Father, how much more do we need that type of focused commitment in our lives? Indeed, we cannot do the *stuff for God* unless we have been inspired and informed by the *stuff from God*. Without a secret life with God our effectiveness in ministry will be short lived or shallow at best.

PRACTICING THE PRESENCE OF GOD

Intentional spiritual formation serves to calibrate our orientation to the love, truth and presence of God so we can live the life Jesus made possible. This includes a relentless surrender to the reigning presence of the indwelling Christ. This is not an esoteric dream, but a very practical and tangible way of living in the real world under the real influence of God, which affects all we do every day. We must resist the tendency to compartmentalize our spiritual life from the rest of our life, no matter how tempting that may be. As Henri Nouwen says, "The spiritual life is not a life before, after, or beyond our everyday

---

108 Willard, *Spirit of the Disciplines*, 5.

existence. No, the spiritual life can only be real when it is lived in the midst of the pains and joys of the here and now."[109]

Historically, those who wrote about this life described it in a variety of ways. Most notably is the classic work of Brother Lawrence entitled, *The Practice of the Presence of God.*[110] This man's unique testimony is propelled by his ambition to live in constant awareness of God's presence. He committed himself to focusing on God in continual conversation—all day every day. Whenever his mind would wander from the reality of God with him, he would immediately realign his sights upon the Lord. Any distractions were dealt with quickly in God's abundant grace, never allowing his failings to derail him from his most joyful aspiration—to live in unshakable communion with God.

For Brother Lawrence, there was no difference in how he experienced God's presence, whether he was seeking God during devotions or walking through the noises and activities of his daily routine. He writes, "My set times of prayer are not different from other times of the day. Although I do retire to pray (because it is the direction of my superior), I do not need such retirement, nor do I ask for it because my greatest business does not divert me from God."[111]

Unlike Brother Lawrence, I cannot claim to not need my daily time set apart each morning to center my mind and heart on God. My experience is that this routine is critical to my spiritual well-being all day long. And I am learning to celebrate the movement toward a sustained, devoted life that is fixed on Christ more than just the fulfillment of my devotional habits. And it is God's continuous presence that makes this possible, since he promises, "I will never leave you nor forsake you.... I am with you always...."[112]

---

[109] Henri Nouwen, *Making All Things New* (San Francisco: Harper Publications, 1981), 21.
[110] Brother Lawrence, *The Practice of the Presence of God* (Beaumont, Texas: The Seed Sowers, 1978).
[111] Lawrence, 47.
[112] Hebrews 13:5; Matthew 28:20

For me, a significant way to "practice the presence of God" is to recognize, enjoy, and obey the Lord moment by moment. Too often we miss God in the *here and now* because we are either thinking regretfully about the past or worrying anxiously about the future. Kingdom living means knowing and enjoying God in the *present moment*. Thomas Kelly refers to this as a "continuously renewed immediacy."[113] Jean Vanier describes the practicality of this perspective when he writes:

> Daily life is only nourishing when we have discovered the wisdom of the present moment and the presence of God in small things. It is only nourishing when we have given up fighting reality and accepting it, discovering the message and gift of the moment.... We stop looking to the future; we take time to live. We are no longer in a hurry because we have discovered that there is a gift and grace in the present of the bookkeeping, the meetings, the chores, and the welcome.[114]

Being attentive to God *each moment* of the day is how we are meant to live. It's how we are intended to work, play, rest, worship, minister—in short, how we experience the life Jesus made possible.

COME AS YOU ARE

The purest motive for pursuing spiritual growth is our love for God and our desire to be more like Jesus. This is how we respond to God's call to follow him. To be like Christ means to love what he loves, say what he would say, and do what he would do if he were here in our place. I heard Dallas Willard once say that we want Christ's instincts

---

[113] Thomas Kelly, *A Testament of Devotion* (San Francisco: Harper & Brothers, 1941), 5.
[114] Jean Vanier, *Community and Growth* (New York: Paulist Press, 1989), 170.

to be our "first response,"[115] because indeed our lives were intended, even destined to become like the life of Jesus. This destiny means that our reactions become habitually Christ-like, and so much so that no matter what life brings we automatically respond as Christ would in the unplanned moments.

To repeatedly respond as Jesus would, we must know and experience God's love and empowering presence on a regular basis. This must be more than a theology only; it must be our 'knee-ology', our knee-jerk reaction to life—experientially knowing that we are the beloved sons and daughters of God. This is not something we can 'claim', but only something we can 'encounter'. When Jesus said, "…this is eternal life, that they may know you, the only true God, and Jesus Christ, whom you have sent" (John 17:3), He was revealing that to experientially know God is the core of our life with him.

While experientially knowing God is a critical aspect of the life Jesus made possible, we don't always experience his presence in the same way or intensity throughout our lives. I have personally endured a number of dry seasons in my relationship with God, times when I found it difficult to sense his loving presence and peace. Some of these seasons have come from extended times of ministry that have left me worn out; others have been the consequence of focusing more on something or someone than I had focused on Jesus, or because of gauging my success more by how I was *doing* than who I was *being*. And when I finally realized that I was getting robbed of the life God designed for me, it helped to remember that my identity as God's beloved is a never changing reality and that, whether I feel his presence or not, he is always near, always with me. Recalling this does not guarantee that the dry spell will end, but it reminds us that we have a home to which we can return anytime.

---

[115] Dallas Willard, Lecture notes from the Fuller Theological Seminary Doctor of Ministry course GM720: Spirituality and Ministry, Pasadena, CA, August 4-15, 1997.

One morning during a particularly parched and dry season, I was struggling to sense God's presence. I began to meditate on the mystery of the Trinity. After a few minutes of contemplation, I sensed the Father saying, "I give you my love." Then Jesus said, "I give you my righteousness." Soon after I sensed the Spirit whisper, "I give you my power." And then with one voice I heard the triune God say, "With these, come and abide!" Discovering afresh God's earnest invitation to be with him, gaining awareness of his presence with me became relatively easy. If we could only see God as he really is and what he has truly provided for us, we would not hesitate to approach him as we are—whether we are in a good or sinful place, whether we feel full or broken and dry! The truth is that the Father loves us and always wants us to run to him, to be held in his arms of love. The truth about Jesus is that he has paid the price for all our sins and failures, and has destroyed the barrier to intimacy with him, opening the doorway to the Kingdom for all who would repent, believe, and enter in. The truth about the Spirit is that he is always with us, and His anointing presence brings us supernatural power and comfort. And it's this Triune God who knows everything about us, yet still invites us to, "Come" (see Matt. 11:28).

Wherever we are in our spiritual journey, we must draw near to the God of all grace just as we are. He accepts our prayers and devotion no matter what our circumstances or condition may be. It is a ploy of Satan to short circuit our coming to God by making us focus on not being "spiritual enough." What a trap! Because of God's mercy, we can start right where we are today, holding nothing back that's in our hearts. God will not be shocked by even the darkest places, and when we come to our awesome God of mercy just as we are, that is when his power is ushered into our lives, enabling us to change and grow. As Jesus said, "Live in me. Make your home in me just as I do in you.... When you're joined with me and I with you, the relation intimate and organic, the harvest is sure to be abundant. Separated, you can't produce a thing" (John 15:4-5, *The Message*).

POWER, SPIRITUAL FORMATION, AND THE SUPERNATURAL LIFE

As already mentioned, there is a critical link between the power of God and his Kingdom. Thus, without the activation of God's power in our lives, Kingdom living remains only an aspiration. As the apostle Paul said, "The Kingdom of God is not a matter of talk, but of power" (1 Corinthians 4:20). Jesus has opened the way for anyone to *enter*, *abide in*, and *extend* the Kingdom of God, which is the "good news" that Jesus came proclaiming.

Power to Enter the Kingdom

We only enter the Kingdom through Jesus Christ; he alone is the way to the Father (see John 14:6). The apostle Paul added, "I am not ashamed of the Gospel, because it is the power of God for salvation" (Romans 1:16). God's power is necessary for us to be saved, and entering the Kingdom is clearly dependent on it. Yet this power is not limited to the "good news" that saves us *from hell* and transfers our citizenship *to heaven*, though this is included. What makes the "good news" so good is that, through Jesus Christ, God has provided his power to all that follow him so that they might truly know him and live under his Kingdom rule—*here and now!* And we can expect God's in-breaking power to touch down in our lives again and again as we continue to faithfully advance God's Kingdom through acts of courageous obedience. Such power encounters are sometimes described as revival, renewal, or the baptism of the Holy Spirit. But whatever one calls it, the reality of this experience and the power that it imparts is unquestionably necessary to live the life Jesus made possible.[116]

---

[116] For an excellent description of the biblical and historical evidence for this significant spiritual experience, see D. Martyn Lloyd-Jones, *Joy Unspeakable: Power & Renewal in the Holy Spirit* (Harold Shaw Publishers, 1984).

Power to Abide in God's Kingdom

It is God's will that we enter his Kingdom and remain under his reigning presence all our lives. As I heard John Wimber once say, "The way *in* is also the way *on!*" John was referring to the supernatural grace of God that makes all aspects of our life with him possible. God does not intend that we simply visit Kingdom life, but rather that we live in it 24-7, and anything short of this is a truncated view of spirituality. Yet it is only God's power and grace that enables us to remain under Christ's reign and rule. In Colossians 1:9-14, the apostle Paul makes this point (emphasis added):

> For this reason, since the day we heard about you, we have not stopped praying for you and asking God to fill you with the knowledge of his will through all spiritual wisdom and understanding. And we pray this in order that you may live a life worthy of the Lord and may please him in every way: bearing fruit in every good work, growing in the knowledge of God, *being strengthened with all power according to his glorious might so that you may have great endurance and patience*, and joyfully giving thanks to the Father, who has qualified you to share in the inheritance of the saints in the kingdom of light. For he has rescued us from the dominion of darkness and brought us into the kingdom of the Son he loves, in whom we have redemption, the forgiveness of sins.

This is Paul's ordinary prayer for ordinary Christians, that they will be anointed with "all power." Notice that it is the Father who has qualified them for this impartation (v. 12), and part of the purpose of their being strengthened with all power according to his glorious might is so they *may have great endurance...* (v. 11). God's power imparts the supernatural ability to endure in his Kingdom, to abide in Christ, and to live filled with the Spirit's empowering presence for a fruitful life.

Power to Extend the Kingdom

The same power that enables us to enter into God's family and abide in Christ is also meant to flow through us to others so that they may know God and live the life Jesus made possible. After speaking to his disciples for 40 days concerning the Kingdom of God, Jesus said:

> But you will receive power when the Holy Spirit comes on you; and you will be my witnesses in Jerusalem, and in all Judea and Samaria, and to the ends of the earth (Acts 1:8).

It was clear that the Lord was giving them his power to do his work on earth.

Luke records Jesus' last words in Acts 1:8 when he promised to extend Kingdom power before ascending into heaven (see Acts 1:9). The early Christians turned this promise into a ten-day prayer meeting until they experienced God's empowering presence at Pentecost (Acts 1:14, 2:1ff). This unleashed power that launched the church into a radical life-long campaign of advancing the Kingdom of God from that day forward!

This same power that was promised in Scripture to Jesus' first disciples and chronicled throughout church history is still desperately needed today—power to *enter, abide in,* and *extend* God's Kingdom, and it's only this power that transforms us into mature and fruitful followers of Christ.

THE SPIRITUAL HABITS

The spiritual habits or disciplines, as they are typically called, are a primary means of grace that help the serious disciple center on Jesus and access God's transforming presence. Such practices as solitude, silence, contemplation, scripture reflection, worship, and prayer serve to create space for God to work in and through one's life as we seek to live under his reign and rule. These habits also free us to know, enjoy, and obey God in an ever-increasing way, creating an atmosphere where God's voice and presence can be experienced daily, enabling us to take hold of that which Christ has put within our reach. These disciplines offer tangible ways that we can abide with God, and they can be used to open our eyes and ears to what the Father is saying and doing.

Dallas Willard organizes the spiritual disciplines in two groups— the disciplines of *abstinence* and the disciplines of *engagement*.[117] I find this helpful because the disciplines of abstinence position us for transformation by *subtracting* something from our lives, while the disciplines of engagement position us for transformation by *adding* something to our lives. The disciplines of abstinence consist of such things as solitude, silence, fasting, frugality, chastity, secrecy, and sacrifice, while the disciplines of engagement include study, worship, celebration, service, prayer, fellowship, confession, and submission.

A thoughtful balance of the disciplines of abstinence and engagement can be likened to a healthy diet with proper portions of protein, fat, and carbohydrates, or as Dallas Willard writes, they are like our need to inhale and exhale:

> Abstinence and engagement are the outbreathing and inbreathing of our spiritual lives, and we require disciplines for both movements. Roughly speaking, the disciplines of abstinence counteract tendencies to sins of commission, and the disciplines of engagement counteract tendencies to sins of omission.... A proper abstinence actually breaks the hold of improper engagements so that the soul can be properly engaged by God.[118]

---

[117] Willard, *Spirit of the Disciplines*, 158.
[118] Willard, *Spirit of the Disciplines*, 175-176.

Evangelicals today tend to emphasize the disciplines of engagement, often to the neglect of the disciplines of abstinence. This emphasis creates an imbalance that impairs spiritual vision and vitality, and also contributes to burnout. My wife and I have seen this happen around the world as we connect with weary missionaries who are doing "God's work" non-stop. We also frequently discover this in coaching leaders and church planters. While many are working hard to make their ministry a success, they are often drying up on the inside and swimming in the shallow end of experiencing God's presence and power.

Such an imbalance should not surprise us, as our professional equipping centers offer much in the realm of gaining theological knowledge and ministry skills, but usually little in terms of practical spiritual formation. In light of this, it is encouraging to see a growing interest and commitment to a more balanced view of spiritual formation in a number of our training institutions.

Reclaiming the Neglected Spiritual Disciplines

While any discipline may contribute powerfully to the formation of a disciple, there are three significant disciplines of abstinence that are often lost in the loud and busy lives of many contemporary believers. These include solitude, silence and centering prayer.

Solitude

Solitude is the proactive choice to break free of the ordinary demands of life in order to be alone with God. Considered by some to be the primary discipline essential for healthy spiritual formation,[119] this practice frees us from the grip of distractions and attachments—setting the stage for fruitful practice of the other disciplines.

Jesus offers a premier example of spending time alone with the Father in solitude,[120] and he also called his disciples to get away to be

---

[119] cf., Willard, *Spirit of the Disciplines*, 161.
[120] For example, Matthew 26:39; Mark 1:35; Luke 4:42; 5:16; 6:12.

alone with him—even in the midst of a successful ministry. Jesus apparently knew that in the clamor and demands of serving him, it is easy to lose perspective. Thus, solitude is imperative not only for our own personal health, but also to provide space to allow the First thing to remain the First thing. Mark records one such situation:

> The apostles gathered around Jesus and reported to him all they had done and taught. Then, because so many people were coming and going that they did not even have a chance to eat, he said to them, "Come with me by yourselves to a quiet place and get some rest" (Mark 6:30-31).

Solitude not only provides physical rest, but it also exposes our issues and gives the Lord time and space to speak to us, touch us, and realign our hearts and minds with his. That's why Henri Nouwen called solitude the "furnace of transformation,"[121] giving this testimony:

> In solitude I get rid of my scaffolding: no friends to talk with, no telephone calls to make, no meeting to attend, no music to entertain, no books to distract, just me—naked, vulnerable, weak, sinful, deprived, broken—nothing. It is this nothingness that I have to face in my solitude, a nothingness so dreadful that everything in me wants to run to my friends, my work, and my distractions so that I can forget my nothingness and make myself believe that I am worth something. But that is not all. As soon as I decide to stay in my solitude, confusing ideas, disturbing images, wild fantasies, and weird associations jump about in my mind like monkeys in a banana tree. Anger and greed begin to show their ugly faces. I give long, hostile speeches to my enemies and dream lustful dreams in which I am wealthy, influential, and very attractive—

---

121 Henri Nouwen, *The Way of the Heart* (New York: Harper, 1981), 25.

or poor, ugly, and in need of immediate consolation. Thus, I try again to run from the dark abyss of my nothingness and restore my false self in all its vainglory. The task is to persevere in my solitude, to stay in my cell until all my seductive visitors get tired of pounding on my door and leave me alone."[122]

This much-needed time to be alone with God does not just happen without dedicated intention and effort. When God says, "Be still and know that I am God" (Psalm 46:10), he is inviting us into a place where our heart can be quieted, and solitude is one way to respond to that directive. David described his need this way:

My heart is not proud, O Lord, my eyes are not haughty; I do not concern myself with great matters or things too wonderful for me. But I have stilled and quieted my soul; like a weaned child with its mother, like a weaned child is my soul within me (Psalm 131:1-2).

In this passage, we are warned against taking ourselves too seriously and being preoccupied as we approach God in our time of solitude. We are to still and quiet our souls. Though not without focused effort, this is possible for every person in relationship with God. The Psalmist tells us that the effect of this could be compared to "a weaned child with its mother." A weaned child does not *have* to be with his or her mother, as was necessary while being nursed. Instead, this child abides in the mother's embrace because he or she desires to, motivated by love. Surely God longs for us to relate to him in a similar way. The Divine Lover relishes the unhurried time we spend in his presence—not because we have to or need to, but because we want to be with him.

Years ago, while I was meditating on this Psalm, the door to my study opened and, as often happened, my youngest son, Caleb, entered

---

122 Nouwen, *Way of the Heart*, 27-28.

the room. He walked over and stood next to me; he then moved in closer and leaned against my side. I waited for the inevitable request— for something to eat or some help from me—but none came. Because I was in the middle of something, I wanted to attend to Caleb's need so I could send him on his way, but Caleb just stood next to me in silence. After a few minutes, I realized that we were experiencing a Psalm 131 moment. Caleb was drawing near for no other reason than simply to be with me. It pains me to think that I almost missed this tender, love-encounter! There were no words, just a few wonderful moments of warmth and togetherness. As we shared our enjoyment of one another in the stillness, we both communicated powerfully our love for one another in a way that no activity or words could. Such is the mystery of solitude.

In the same way, the Psalmist talks about intentionally stilling and quieting his *soul*—that is, his inner world. Though not without focused effort, becoming settled and centered in our relationship with God is the major purpose of solitude. The mysterious impact of solitude is experienced when, in the quiet, we experience God's presence and align with his Kingdom in us. This mystery cannot be over-emphasized because, while solitude may seem unproductive, it is often the very best way to spend our time. This reality is emphasized in the story of Jesus and two sisters, Mary and Martha.

> As Jesus and his disciples were on their way, he came to a village where a woman named Martha opened her home to him. She had a sister called Mary, who sat at the Lord's feet listening to what he said. But Martha was distracted by all the preparations that had to be made. She came to him and asked, 'Lord, don't you care that my sister has left me to do the work by myself? Tell her to help me!' (Luke 10:38-40).

Here Mary was found sitting with Jesus, listening to all he had to say. She had stilled and quieted her soul to experience God and take in his words. On the other hand, Martha was distracted by her service.

She had miscalculated what was truly important to Jesus and to her own soul, and, therefore, she missed the chance to connect with the Lord because she was anxiously preparing a meal Jesus never ordered! She was further distracted by the resentment in her heart toward her sister, Mary—whom Martha considered to be wasting time sitting at the feet of Jesus when so much needed to be done. But in fact, it was Mary who discerned Jesus' desire to have her near, stilled in his presence and attentive to his voice. In a world addicted to activity and performance, we must live in light of these corrective words Jesus spoke to Martha:

> Martha, Martha, you are worried and upset about many things, but only one thing is needed. Mary has chosen what is better, and it will not be taken away from her (Luke 10:41-42).

Solitude is that place where we are given time to sit and listen to our Lord. And while solitude does yield fruit that can be seen later in service, that is not its purpose. I've learned to embrace solitude as a way to settle my soul and clarify my vision, but still my own internal 'Martha' often protests and demands that I move on to something more directly productive. I guess solitude wouldn't be called a discipline if it didn't require intention and effort. But the resulting fruit of becoming centered in the truth and love of God is so worth the occasional struggle.

Silence

The second important discipline of abstinence is silence, which tends to complete and intensify solitude.[123] This fundamental discipline has two forms. The first is that of quiet—meaning we need to find a space that is absent of as many distractions as possible. Sometimes we don't realize the negative consequence of living in a noisy world until we experience an extended time of silence. Finding an occasional

---

123 Nouwen, *The Way of the Heart*, 43.

escape from the common noises of life is an important step in cultivating a sense of God's presence and our ability to hear his voice. Isaiah 30:15 says, "This is what the Sovereign Lord, the Holy One of Israel, says: 'In repentance and rest is your salvation, *in quietness* and trust is your strength...'" In silence, we experience God in a way that strengthens us for the life that Jesus made possible.

Today, the average person is over stimulated with a myriad of sights and sounds. With computers, iPads, email, Smartphones, Facebook, Instagram, and Twitter, it has become nearly impossible to be alone and silent. And the human body responds to and absorbs these stimuli whether we know it or not. For me, I've learned not to check my email or social media until *after* I've spent time with God in the morning, since a "quick look" often turns into a long distraction that's hard to pull away from. Incessant distraction is no small issue today, and it behooves us to commit to a plan that provides extended time of solitude and silence—which may require observing an occasional 'technology fast' to break any addiction to "staying in touch."

The discipline of silence first entails finding a place where external noise is minimal, but the second form involves deciding to occasionally *stop speaking*. The Bible gives us this exhortation:

> Guard your steps when you go to the house of God. Go near to listen rather than to offer the sacrifice of fools, who do not know that they do wrong. Do not be quick with your mouth; do not be hasty in your heart to utter anything before God. God is in heaven and you are on earth, so let your words be few (Ecclesiastes 5:1-2).

Our tongues can easily become a source of power, control, or manipulation, but the discipline of silence is one way we learn to master them. Excessive speech can be used to adjust one's image, especially when we believe we've been wronged. The discipline of silence forces us to let God be our vindicator. The heavy burden of constantly defending and justifying ourselves is lifted in silence and left in the hands of God, the One who said, "Come to me, all you who are weary and burdened, and I will give you rest" (Matthew 11:28). As Henri Nouwen points out:

> Sometimes it seems that our many words are more an expression of our doubt than of our faith. It is as if we are not sure that God's Spirit can touch the hearts of people: we have to help him out, and with many words convince others of his power.[124]

I have found a tangible way to practice this discipline in the exercise of giving up "the last word," even when I have an impressionable point to make. The discipline of silence can also be practiced when questions are raised and you have something important to offer. Instead of immediately answering, try refraining and allowing others to respond first. I often face this challenge in staff meetings and small groups, but when I hold back—even when I have something *really good* to say—inevitably someone else offers a similar idea to mine. Now I'm learning to be happy because the important points were made, not that I was the one who made them. This helps me grow in the reality that my security and significance are not dependent on what I do or say—even if that was making a contribution.

At my Baccalaureate ceremony at Fuller Seminary, Dr. Archibald Hart addressed a room full of doctoral graduates with these opening words, "You talk too much!" I knew he was right. Many disciples, especially leaders, talk much and listen little—not only to others but also to the Lord himself. Nouwen addresses this when he writes, "Silence prevents us from being suffocated by our wordy world, and teaches us to speak only the Word of God."[125] Similarly, Richard Foster writes, "Only when we learn to be truly silent are we able to speak the word that is needed *when* it is needed."[126] There is a time to be silent and a time to speak (see Eccl. 3:7), and the discipline of silence can

---

[124] Nouwen, *The Way of the Heart*, 54.
[125] Nouwen, *The Way of the Heart*, 91.
[126] Foster, *Celebration of Discipline*, 102.

show us the way.

<u>Centering Prayer</u>

"Centering prayer" is a potent discipline that can be incorporated into times of solitude and silence. Here the goal is not to produce anything or to receive something from God. We simply come into God's presence intending to do nothing…with no agenda, no books, no prayer requests, *nothing* that would distract us from simply being with him. It sounds strange, doesn't it? But the seeming pointlessness of this discipline is the point! During centering prayer we enter God's presence to simply be with him—without demands or expectations. This contradicts the false belief that everything done in the name of "spiritual formation" must result in producing something tangible by this world's standard. This is especially true for those in vocational ministry. The purpose of centering prayer is not to get something done, but simply to *be with God.*

Most mornings I try to spend 15 minutes of uninterrupted time in centering prayer. I often practice this after reading scripture that has somehow stirred my heart. First, I select a simple meditative phrase from the passage that keeps me present to God. For example, when reading Psalm 23 recently, this phrase caught my attention: "The Lord is my shepherd, I shall not be in want." I then meditated on the phrase, "You are my sufficiency," and sat with God—eyes closed and heart focused on the all-sufficient One. When a random thought would enter my mind and distract me (usually something I needed to do later that day), I simply re-centered my attention on the all-sufficient One by repeating the phrase, "You are my sufficiency." Gradually, I became settled and centered on God himself. These times are precious and have proven to be an essential habit for maintaining my awareness of God's presence throughout the day.

Let me distinguish between the Christian discipline of centering prayer and a form of meditation practiced by many eastern religions. In the latter type, the purpose of meditation is to empty one's mind of all thoughts and go deeper within oneself. This can lead to deception. The purpose of centering prayer, however, is to fill our minds with a truth revealed by God, which serves to center our souls and focus our minds on God's presence.

Centering prayer has often indirectly resulted in many blessings from God, including spiritual rest, peace, security, mental clarity, increased creativity and a meaningful sense of belonging. What a paradox! I receive the most of God in a context where I intentionally request nothing from him, except the privilege to be with him. Despite all of these positive results, the intangible nature of this discipline still requires me to approach centering prayer as a discipline, as opposed to the very tangible, relentless and loud demands of my iPhone reminders and "To Do" lists. Centering prayer remains an act of faith motivated by love.

THE DANGER OF LEGALISM

Disciplines are imperative for a healthy relationship with God, yet they must never become an end in themselves, nor a ruler by which we measure our spiritual performance. Rather, the spiritual disciplines are and will always be a *means* to the End—abiding with God. The disciplines are designed to "bring us into more effective cooperation with Christ and his Kingdom."[127] They are a way of sowing to the Spirit, planting us in 'Kingdom soil' where God can work to grow and transform us. "By themselves the spiritual disciplines can do nothing; they can only get us to the place where something can be done. They are God's means of grace."[128] But whenever the disciplines are turned into an end, in and of themselves, a fruitless legalism soon takes root.

The story of Zacchaeus (recorded in Luke 19:1-10) serves as a useful illustration for using the spiritual disciplines effectively.[129]

---

[127] Dallas Willard, *The Spirit of the Disciplines* (San Francisco: Harper & Row Publishers, 1988), 156.

[128] Richard Foster, *Celebration of Discipline*, Revised ed. (San Francisco: Harper Collins, 1988), 7.

[129] I apologize ahead of time for the hermeneutical license taken in making this point!

Jesus entered Jericho and was passing through. A man was there by the name of Zacchaeus; he was a chief tax collector and was wealthy. He wanted to see who Jesus was, but being a short man he could not because of the crowd. So, he ran ahead and climbed a sycamore-fig tree to see him, since Jesus was coming that way.

When Jesus reached the spot, he looked up and said to him, "Zacchaeus, come down immediately. I must stay at your house today." So, he came down at once and welcomed him gladly.

All the people saw this and began to mutter, "He has gone to be the guest of a 'sinner.' But Zacchaeus stood up and said to the Lord, "Look, Lord! Here and now I give half of my possessions to the poor, and if I have cheated anybody out of anything, I will pay back four times the amount." Jesus said to him, "Today salvation has come to this house, because this man, too, is a son of Abraham. For the Son of Man came to seek and to save what was lost.

Notice that Zacchaeus wanted to see Jesus, to know who he was. But he realized his limitation: he was a short man! Left to himself, he would miss the opportunity to even catch a glimpse of Jesus. So, Zacchaeus did what *he could*: He positioned himself in a tree where it was possible for him to see Jesus and make a meaningful connection with him.

Similarly, when we desire to see God and be closer to him, we must recognize our limitations—our distractibility, character lapses, brokenness, and sin—and intentionally position ourselves so that we can see the Lord more clearly. Like Zacchaeus, it's important that we identify what holds us back and choose the appropriate tree (or discipline) with which to connect meaningfully with the Lord. This is what the spiritual disciplines do: they create space for God to work and speak into our lives.

After Zacchaeus' branch had fulfilled its purpose (helping him meet Jesus), he needed to leave it in order to further develop his relationship with Jesus. How ridiculous to think of Zacchaeus saying, "Oh no, Lord, I must not come down from this branch, for this is what has made it possible for me to connect with you." The connection with Jesus was the point, not the helpful branch!

Soon after leaving the tree, Zacchaeus was able to enjoy Jesus' company and, ultimately, experience the good news of the Kingdom, as Jesus declared, "Today salvation has come to this house". To be sure, Jesus provided what Zacchaeus absolutely *could not* do for himself. God often faithfully and graciously meets us and does what only he can do when: 1) we really desire to see and know him, 2) we position ourselves for him to work in our lives, and 3) we simply obey any directive he gives us.

This story further illustrates the necessity for variety in the use of spiritual disciplines. Imagine if Zacchaeus decided to be stubborn and return to the tree branch that worked last time, but which was nowhere near where Jesus was traveling on his next visit. When your goal and motive is simply to see and know Jesus, you will use whatever means necessary to be with him. We must resist making an idol of any method of spiritual formation. Once you connect with the Lord, then it is time to humbly abide and follow him wherever he may lead.

Satisfaction with mere fulfillment of a devotional routine is a deceptive trap. I greatly appreciate Brother Lawrence's emphasis on not making any devotional method an end in itself:

> You will also find it necessary to lay aside some forms of devotion, even if they are good ones. Such devotions are only the means to the end. They were given to you to bring you to Christ's presence. Once you are in his presence, the forms are meaningless. When we are in his presence this *is* the end; it is

therefore of no value to return to the means. Persevere to be with him.[130]

To summarize, the purpose for practicing spiritual disciplines is encountering *God himself*, not doing the disciplines per se. Furthermore, the goal is not only to connect with God *during* the discipline itself, but also to remain aligned with him through the rest of the day—being continuously aware of his abiding presence.

GRACE IS NOT OPPOSED TO EFFORT

We absolutely need to avoid legalism. But many people seem to have reacted to legalism—and its deadly burden of false guilt—by embracing an equally crippling mentality: that a grace-based spirituality does not require effort or discipline. The truth is, "grace is not opposed to *effort* but to *earning*."[131] As Nouwen states, "A spiritual life without discipline is impossible."[132] Like any other relationship, effort is required if I'm to grow in my relationship with God. We must learn to focus, listen, and be present with the ones we love. Consider the apostle Peter's exhortation:

> For this very reason, *make every effort* to add to your faith goodness; and to goodness, knowledge; and to knowledge, self-control; and to self-control, perseverance; and to perseverance, godliness; and to godliness, brotherly kindness; and to brotherly kindness, love. For if you possess these qualities in increasing measure, they will keep you from being ineffective and unproductive in your knowledge of our Lord Jesus Christ (2 Peter 1:5-8, emphasis added).

---

130 Brother Lawrence, *The Practice of the Presence of God*, 70.
131 Willard, Lecture notes.
132 Nouwen, *Making All Things New*, 66.

In his book, *The Cost of Discipleship*, Dietrich Bonhoeffer offers a prophetic message to our generation—a generation that largely insists on personal rights and privileges without any equivalent responsibility. He calls this distortion "cheap grace,"[133] and describes it as "grace without discipleship, grace without the cross."[134] It is a grievous condition into which many in the contemporary church have succumbed. Cheap grace is both a theological and a practical problem. Through the years I have heard several popular Christian leaders speak sarcastically concerning basic issues of sanctification and the focus on spiritual disciplines, all in the name of "grace." I have even heard jokes about being "addicted to grace." Yet, in the context, the undercurrent seems to be an aversion to the cost of discipleship.

We must never succumb to the heresy of legalism—nurturing a religious spirit that focuses on spiritual performance and perfection. But on the other hand, we must not allow the fear of being perceived as legalistic or religious to keep us from practicing real grace, which indeed is costly. Ironically, attempting to combat legalism by practicing and promoting cheap grace actually places us under the worst kind of legalism—religion without a true abiding relationship with Jesus, who is the perfect fulfillment of the law. Bonhoeffer sums up the seriousness of this when he writes, "The word of cheap grace has been the ruin of more Christians than any commandment of works."[135] Again, true grace is not opposed to effort, but to earning. Grace is not only God's unmerited acceptance, but also his divine enablement to fully embrace and live the life Jesus made possible.

---

[133] Dietrich Bonhoeffer, *The Cost of Discipleship* (New York, Macmillan Publishing, 1978), 45.
[134] Bonhoeffer, 47.
[135] Bonhoeffer, 59.

ABIDING WITH GOD ALL DAY LONG

A life of devotion to abiding with God opens us to a flow of blessing, as described in Psalm 89:15-16:

> Blessed are those who have learned to acclaim you,
> Who walk in the light of your presence, O Lord.
> They rejoice in your name all day long;
> they exult in your righteousness.

Here God promises to bless those devoted to a lifestyle of intentional spiritual formation—those who rejoice in the name of God all day long and exult in his righteousness. This is a way of life that focuses upon God. This approach to life must be *learned*, and requires tangible, intentional effort. The blessed disciple must *learn* to acclaim the Lord, which in this context can mean, "to greet God with enthusiastic praise."

Because God never sleeps, it's our joyful privilege to wake up every morning to his presence. This speaks of beginning one's day with praise and attention on the goodness and greatness of God, which is what spiritual formation is all about. I recall an Episcopal priest describing his habit of getting out of bed in the morning with hands raised and voice declaring, "I rise in the strength of the Holy Trinity!" That's a good example of acclaiming the Lord. The blessed disciple in Psalm 89 not only greets God in the morning, but also goes into the rest of the day in the light of God's presence. This is the Kingdom lifestyle that the spiritual disciplines both encourage and facilitate, allowing us to be blessed and devoted—morning, noon, and night. Here is a practical example of how such a lifestyle could be approached:

Morning

It is beneficial to have a specific time at the beginning of the day to align one's mind and heart to God. This time doesn't necessarily have to be lengthy, but it must be focused. Again, it was Jesus' pattern to spend time alone with the Father in the early morning hours. For us, this may include worship, the reading of Scripture and other spiritual literature, prayer, journaling, and time given to centering prayer. Also, praying through one's daily schedule is helpful, envisioning the truth that God will be with you in each moment throughout the day.

Through the Day

Whatever one does in the morning, the goal is to be able to head into the day centered and focused in such a way as to "walk in the light of God's presence." Our aspiration is to remain aligned with the truth and person of God all day long. This will mean refocusing one's mind again and again—as often as it drifts from the awareness of God and his Kingdom among us. A simple prayer—asking for a fresh touch of God's presence, wisdom, and strength—at every transition throughout the day can have a powerful impact on one's ability to abide in God's presence. Taking advantage of any unplanned down time can also be strategic. As my college pastor once said, "Don't waste the five 'minuteses' this life affords you." Instead of fretting when someone is late, harness those moments to ponder a truth that God spoke to you in the morning, or spend time in conversation and praise to God. Perhaps you could even pray for and bless your tardy friend!

Bedtime

Before retiring at night, a brief time of purposeful prayer can serve to keep one's heart focused, full, and free. Don't use bedtime to meditate on stressful, unfinished business, but rather, offer simple, childlike prayers that can include:

- Gratitude—Giving thanks for what God has done and provided throughout the day;

- Confession—Admitting to God any failures in thought, word and deed during the day, and receiving his forgiveness;

- Forgiveness and blessing—Extending forgiveness and blessing to all those who may have offended or wounded you in the course of the day;

- Resolution—A final phrase during evening prayer may also include a resolution to wake up in the morning with the awareness that God is with you, loves you, and that you will purposefully abide with him throughout the next day.

CONCLUSION

The essential ingredient to living the life Jesus made possible is learning to abide with God throughout each day. We can grow in this abiding lifestyle as we make space to hear God's voice and experience his loving and empowering presence all day long. And we must learn to do this in the life we *actually* live, not the one we *wish* we were living. There must be an intentional beginning of this spiritual journey if we are to truly experience the abiding life. If you are not certain your journey has begun, you can make that commitment today. Take a few minutes right now to ask God's Spirit to help you tangibly encounter the truth of His gracious love and abiding presence. If it is your desire to abide with Christ, I suggest you begin by embracing the truth that the Father loves you, the Son has made the way for such a life to happen, and that the Spirit's empowering presence in and through you can, and will, make all things new!

CHAPTER 8

MAKING SPACE FOR FRIENDS

Two are better than one.... If one falls down,
his friend can help him up.
But pity the man who falls and has no one to help
him up!... Though one may be overpowered,
two can defend themselves. A cord of three strands
is not quickly broken. (Ecclesiastes 4:9-12)

Without community, there is no Christianity.[136]

Not long ago, I was teaching a weeklong course at a YWAM (Youth With A Mission) Discipleship Training School. The purpose of the YWAM DTS is to prepare young adults to spend several months together in a uniquely intense missional equipping environment. These emerging missionaries were living in close proximity and spending many hours a day together, but after I spoke on maintaining healthy relationships, several shared privately that they were struggling with loneliness. It was surprising to hear this from these young adults living in a Christian, communal setting. On the other hand it reminded me of the truth Nouwen shares about loneliness:

> "When we are lonely we perceive ourselves as isolated individuals surrounded, perhaps, by many people, but not really part of any supporting or

---

[136] Gilbert Bilezikian, *Community 101* (Grand Rapids, MI: Zondervan Publishing House, 1997), 35.

nurturing community. Loneliness is without doubt one of the most widespread diseases of our time."[137]

Yes, even in a technologically interconnected world, loneliness remains one of the most common ailments disclosed by college students and people in the church. They complain about feeling alone, yet they're simultaneously too afraid to connect with others. Ironically, the intimacy we long for is often the very thing we fear most. And understandably so, because most of us know that connecting with others—even in the body of Christ—often brings pain with it. Past wounding makes it easier to maintain a safe distance rather than taking the risk to get close to people again.

Despite our fears, every human heart deeply longs to be intimately connected with God and others. When we circumvent that longing, we discover that no coping mechanism—regardless of how sophisticated it may be—can replace what authentic relationship with others can do for the human heart. According to God's word, the members of Christ's body are meant to be interdependently fastened together (consider 1 Cor. 12:14ff). It's God himself who designed us to move from isolation into intentional community with those who love Jesus—for the glory of God!

Furthermore, scripture also says that the quality of our relationships with others is a visible measurement of the quality of our relationship with God.[138]

> "If you want a good litmus test of your spiritual growth, simply examine the nature and quality of your relationships with others. Are you more loving, more compassionate, more patient, more understanding, more caring, more giving, more forgiving than you were a year ago? If you cannot answer these kinds of questions in the affirmative and, especially, if others

---

[137] Henri Nouwen, *Making All Things New*, 32
[138] For example, see 1 John 4:20,21

cannot answer them in the affirmative about you, then you need to examine carefully the nature of your spiritual life and growth."[139]

True spirituality is relational at the core. Robert Mulholland addresses this in his definition of spiritual formation: "Spiritual formation is a process of being conformed to the image of Christ *for the sake of others.*"[140] I like to say that the Christian life is actually a relational miracle between God and man, and this miracle is meant to be experienced in our relationships with others.

Unfortunately, the Western church has propagated a Christianity that normalizes a privatized relationship with God. An example of this erroneous ecclesiology can be heard in comments I have often heard like the following, "All that counts is your relationship with God, and that is something just between you and him." This mentality promotes a lie that a person's relationship with God is in no way connected to their relationships with others, and vice versa—a fallacy that has produced great dysfunction in the body of Christ today. The evangelical church has often focused on the work of ministry while neglecting the need for functional community It is disheartening to consider how much religious activity has been birthed outside of an abiding relationship with God that is lived within the context of intentional, covenantal relationships with other Christ-followers.[141] It's an erroneous idea to believe we can come to spiritual maturity alone. "Much of what passes for spiritual formation these days is a very privatized, individualized experience. It does not enliven and enrich the body of Christ, nor is it vitally dependent upon the body of Christ

---

[139] M. Robert Mulholland Jr., *Invitation To A Journey: A Roadmap for Spiritual Formation* (Downers Grove, IL: InterVarsity Press, 1993), 42.

[140] Mulholland, *Invitation To A Journey*, 12.

[141] Concerning a theology of the visible church, Simon Chan writes, "This is one of the least developed areas of Protestant thought, especially among evangelicals." Simon Chan, *Spiritual Theology: A Systematic Study of the Christian Life* (Downers Grove, Illinois: InterVarsity Press, 1998), 103.

for its own wholeness."[142] A theology that allows relational disconnection—and even makes it a virtuous option—is not consistent with God's Word or God's nature.

Personally, it's not difficult for me to admit that I deeply need God. That is evident to me every day. But I'm continually learning what it means to need other followers of Jesus in a healthy way. The Word teaches that authentic connection with believers is not meant to be co-dependent or enmeshed but, rather, supportive and healing. Our relationships with other believers are intended to enrich our love for God, just as our relationships with God are meant to intensify our love for others—including family, friends, and those outside the body of Christ. Love for God and others is interrelated, as the apostle John said:

> We love because he first loved us. If anyone says, "I love God," yet hates his brother, he is a liar. For anyone who does not love his brother, whom he has seen, cannot love God, whom he has not seen. And he has given us this command: Whoever loves God must also love his brother (1 John 4:19-21).

But it can be challenging for many to find their way toward healthy community—even for Christians who desire it. As we grow closer to others, we're often met with—and required to navigate through—disappointment and heartache. Consequently, it can appear easier to avoid the pain and consider just "going it alone," but this is not God's intent, and our aloneness will never bring satisfaction to the human heart. As Jean Vanier writes:

> Perhaps it is too late. Maybe we do not have the inner force to live community. Perhaps we are all too broken and the inner pain too great. But somewhere, in the heart of humanity today, there is a cry coming from our own loneliness and the injustices and pain of

---

[142] Mulholland, *Invitation To A Journey*, 14.

our own world: a cry for community, for belonging, for togetherness, and for love.[143]

Our cry for community comes from God himself. He put this desire in our hearts and wired us with a longing to know intimacy with him and one another. This yearning is a gift, and Jesus Christ has put fulfillment of the desire within our reach. One of the central reasons Jesus came was to make it possible for his disciples to have an abundant life, a life lived "to the full" (John 10:10). But this fruitful life can only be developed and sustained within supportive Christian environments. And therein lies the strategic purpose of community: to provide safe places where disciples can grow and multiply through consistent encouragement and accountability. Because of its critical role in forming disciples and advancing God's Kingdom, spiritual leaders must contend for the cultivation of authentic community as a central goal.

The fact is that we need one another to live life as God intended, and this reality was first revealed in the Garden of Eden when God said, "It is not good for man to be alone" (Genesis 2:18). Interestingly, when God said that, he and Adam were already enjoying a significant, intimate relationship. Yet by God's appraisal, the situation was 'not good,' because God knew that the "creation of his image required a plurality of persons (cf., Genesis 1:26,27). Therefore, the woman was created to 'help' the man out of his aloneness so that together they would form the community of oneness."[144] This has always been God's plan: to address aloneness by providing relational connection (just as he did with Adam). Therefore, God has given us marriage, family, and the Church as communities to help us grow as well as minister to the aloneness of our hearts.

---

[143] Jean Vanier, *From Brokenness to Community* (New York: Paulist Press, 1992), 34-35.
[144] Bilezikian, *Community 101*, 20.

WHAT IS CHRISTIAN COMMUNITY?

Christian community can be described as the activity and fruit of two or more people meeting together in Jesus' name. It arises when we are genuinely connected with others for the purpose of encouraging mutual connection with God. Community is what makes it possible for that connection to take place, but it certainly is possible to participate in being with others without a genuine connection. That is why it is not uncommon to hear believers say, "I am having difficulty opening up and feeling connected with my small group at First *Community* Church." The fact is that community is more of a mystery to be experienced than a program to be designed. Larry Crabb describes this when he says, "Wherever there is supernatural togetherness and Spirit-directed movement, there is the church—a spiritual community…. Managers try to explain it and call themselves theologians. Mystics enjoy it and become lovers."[145] However difficult it may be to describe, being authentically connected with other Christ followers is essential for living the life Jesus made possible.

THE COMMUNITY WITHIN OUR REACH

Having been the pastor of a fairly large church, I've occasionally heard people say that they aren't experiencing community during our Sunday morning services. But the kind of intimate connection they desire rarely happens in a gathering of hundreds of people. Instead, this dynamic happens when we pursue the "community within the crowd." The diagram below describes how our faith community sought to cultivate relationships in our congregation by viewing connection through a lens of what we called the "Concentric Circles of Community." While *Intimate Community* provides the deepest level of connection for people (the level many people long for), the other

---

[145] Larry Crabb, *The Safest Place on Earth* (Nashville: Word Publishing, 1999).

expressions of community are equally valid. In fact, the wider concentric circles serve to put the narrower circles of deeper relationships within our reach. Let's take a look at what each level is and how it functions, starting with the largest circle.

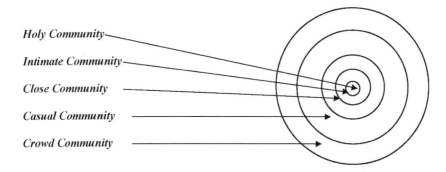

Crowd Community

Crowd Community happens when large numbers of believers gather either occasionally or regularly for worship, inspiration, celebration, and instruction. The purpose of Crowd Community is not to experience intimacy with others, but rather to obtain fresh vision and inspiration concerning life in the Kingdom of God. Crowd Community is typically more dependent upon a leader than it is participatory in style (consider a typical Sunday morning church service as an example). The large church gatherings at the temple courts in Jerusalem also illustrate Crowd Community in the New Testament (Cf., Acts 2:41-46; 3:11; 4:4; 5:12).

Casual Community

Casual Community is the expression that occurs when people gather occasionally without a specific purpose or covenant that addresses the nature of their relationships. Casual Community settings are ideal for helping people make initial connections and perhaps do something meaningful together. The missional church often utilizes this space to bring believers and not-yet-believers together into relational proximity. This can happen when we invite people to things like a BBQ or a party. People may sincerely enjoy relational togetherness in Casual Community, but it is seldom the kind of place where relationships go deep unless another level of community has already been present.

Close Community

Close Community is the kind of fellowship that can be experienced in a small group that gathers regularly and intentionally. The group size is often between 6-15 participants. Some groups of this kind remain open to new members, while others close after a certain amount of time or when the group reaches a particular size. People may attend several such gatherings. The commitment and stability of these Close Communities often allows a deeper level of fellowship to be achieved (as compared to Crowd or Casual Community), especially when there is covenantal stability in the group.

Intimate Community

Intimate Community is an expression of community most often experienced with only a handful of other dedicated disciples of Jesus. This unmistakable connection enjoyed in the safety of Intimate Community is fashioned by the Holy Spirit through serious commitment and clear covenant. Terry Wardle describes this level of spiritual friendship well when he writes:

> They are not the crowd—that group of strangers you meet daily but do not know beyond formality. They are not the committee—that working group held together by formal structures of organization. No, the necessary people I am describing are the community of believers that comprises your closest companions, intimate friends growing to know one another on their way to knowing God. You need them and they need you. In supporting you along the difficult way of life, they, too, grow in spiritual stature and health. It is an unavoidable

consequence of the interrelationship that belongs to true Christian community. In healthy relationships you and they change.[146]

Holy Community

Holy Community happens when believers fellowship with the Father, Son and Holy Spirit. The Trinity is the true source and center of all Christian community, and intimacy with this Holy Community of perfect love is an answer to Jesus' prayer recorded in John 17:25-26:

> Righteous Father, though the world does not know you, I know you, and they know that you have sent me. I have made you known to them, and will continue to make you known in order that the love you have for me may be in them and that I myself may be in them.

Holy Community is intended to be both the Source and greatest expression of spiritual intimacy that followers of Jesus get to experience.

THE PURPOSE OF COMMUNITY

Encouragement and Accountability

Jesus' real invitation to his followers is for us to become his friends for life, with the goal of becoming increasingly more like him in every area. But the decision of becoming a lifelong apprentice of Jesus does not happen automatically, nor is it an easy commitment to follow. Every would-be disciple needs practical and consistent support along the way. "We should apprentice ourselves to Jesus in a solemn moment, and we should let those around us know that we have done so."[147] Such a solemn communication to other disciples is significant as it's not possible to faithfully follow Christ alone: we need the

---

[146] Terry Wardle, *Draw Close To The Fire*, 149.
[147] Willard, *Divine Conspiracy*, 298.

consistent encouragement and accountability of others who are also moving toward God and the life he made possible.

The following text offers important insights regarding the relationship between encouragement and community:

> Therefore, brothers, since we have confidence to enter the Most Holy Place by the blood of Jesus, by a new and living way opened for us through the curtain, that is, his body, and since we have a great priest over the house of God, *let us* draw near to God with a sincere heart in full assurance of faith, having our hearts sprinkled to cleanse us from a guilty conscience and having our bodies washed with pure water. *Let us* hold unswervingly to the hope we profess, for he who promised is faithful. And *let us* consider how we may spur one another on toward love and good deeds. *Let us* not give up meeting together, as some are in the habit of doing, but *let us* encourage one another—and all the more as you see the Day approaching (Hebrews 10:19-25, emphasis added).

These verses reveal the basis for having a rich spiritual life. Through Christ, God has made it possible to abide under his effective rule, and the five "*let us*" exhortations here are nestled between the theological truths that Jesus has both *come* (vv. 19-20) and is *coming again* (v. 25b). Left to ourselves, we tend to let our attention drift to what we have done in the past (which can lead to regret or pride) or to what we propose to do in the future (which can lead to ambition or worry). Rather than focus on oneself, Christ's disciples are to learn to contemplate and live in light of what God has done, is doing, and has promised to do. We are encouraged to endeavor to live in the present moment under the influence of God's reign, seeing life on earth from his perspective.

To "hold unswervingly to the hope that we profess" (v. 23) is another way to express the reality of "practicing the presence of

God."[148] We "hold unswervingly" when we gain stability in our walk with God, not swerving in and out of the hope that God gives. Our faithful God has not called us to simply *visit* the Kingdom but rather to *live* in the Kingdom with all of its power and promises. That lifestyle can only happen because of what God has done to enable us to "hold unswervingly to the hope that we profess." This possibility was, first of all, put within our reach through the work of Christ that opened the way for us to live in his presence (vv. 19-20). Secondly, this unswerving life is possible because God is forever *with us* to help us along the way (see v. 21). And thirdly, it is possible because God is in charge of the future, and the Day is coming when Jesus will return for his Bride (v. 25). As we meditate on and walk in these truths, our lives become anchored more deeply to the King and his Kingdom—past, present, and future.

However, this Kingdom life does not "just happen" without intentional effort. Notice that the exhortation to "hold unswervingly" is surrounded by the encouragements to "draw near to God" (v. 22), and to "spur one another on toward love and good deeds" (v. 24). A tenacious and passionate pursuit of God in connection with our fellow travelers is essential to thriving in God's Kingdom. Consequently, when it comes to connecting with others, we are exhorted to specifically consider how we will in fact connect. "And let us consider how we may spur one another on toward love and good deeds" (v. 24). We are warned not to "give up meeting together, as some are in the habit of doing" (v. 25), and in Hebrews 3:13 we are told that being negligent in community life will eventually lead to a heart that is hard toward God. That is why we need to consistently meet together and "spur one another on." The purpose of this holy 'nudging' is to keep us moving toward God's love and good deeds, allowing the Lord to work in and through others to encourage us to live faithfully and fully in Jesus. In this kind of community, faithful friends are positioned to

---

[148] As described by Brother Lawrence in his book entitled, *Practicing The Presence of God.*

encourage us to stay the course whenever we grow weary or lose our way.

> When we don't feel like worshipping, the community should carry us along in its worship. When we can't seem to pray, community prayer should enfold us. When the Scripture seems closed for us, the community should keep on reading, affirming and incarnating it around us.[149]

An Incubator of Formation

Intentional community also creates an environment of disclosure that helps us grow. Who we really are and what is truly happening inside of us will eventually be exposed in community life. This relational connection is meant to shape us into the likeness of Jesus— "as iron sharpens iron, so one man sharpens another" (Proverbs 27:17). Yet even in community, we can be tempted to cover up, project, or run from the reality of our own brokenness. Our lack of love and our sin will be exposed in the 'squeeze' of consistent connecting. Apart from such revelation (brought about through truthful community life), a person can continue to live in a self-deceived and pretentious way, not becoming fully mature—or as Paul put it: "attaining to the whole measure of the fullness of Christ" (Eph 4:13).

Community is a major means of grace for revealing our inner selves. "While we were alone, we could believe we loved everyone,"[150] but abiding together in community has a way of divulging the unsettled issues in our heart. For example, I'm learning that my perception of being wronged is only a small part of what truly matters; my *reaction* to being wronged, on the other hand, clearly has the potential to make or break the well-being of my community. A painful encounter in my

---

[149] Mulholland, *Invitation To A Journey*, 146.
[150] Jean Vanier, *Community and Growth*, 26.

community does not create the junk that surfaces from within me, but it does expose it—offering me the environment in which I can discover and deal with the 'log in my own eye'. Here "all the darkness and anger, jealousies and rivalry hidden within our hearts are revealed."[151]

The difficulties encountered in community also serve to drive us to God in a deeper way. Though obviously undesirable, such difficulties are a common occurrence when people spend consistent time together, which can be uncomfortable. Due to this discomfort, it is not rare for people to run away from what they see in the closeness of community or to sabotage these relationships before attempting to discover what God has in mind for them. Connecting with other imperfect people requires us to live near the cross, since community life is really the 'cross life'. The humility of planting the cross in the middle of every relationship means it will not be uncommon to hear someone say, "I'm sorry." And for the other to say, "I forgive you." To live well with others, we must develop a lifestyle of speaking the truth in love, grace and ongoing reconciliation.

LESSONS FROM THE MONASTERY

Monastic communities have offered a peculiar and fruitful expression of intentional community throughout much of Christian history. On numerous occasions, I've been a guest at various religious communities, spending a few days or even a few weeks with them at a time. And while my primary purpose for visiting has been to rest and seek God in solitude, the monks have taught me much about how to live a spiritually supported life in fellowship with others. Though their way of life is different than mine, my heart resonates with their passion

---

[151] Vanier, *From Brokenness To Community*, 29.

to practice the presence of God–while loving God and the others in their covenant community.

A wonderful book by M. Basil Pennington called, *Lessons From The Monastery That Touch Your Life,* offers unusual insight into the spiritual climate of the monastic community.[152] Beyond a general description of community life, Pennington presents practical lessons that can be adapted and applied to our more familiar expressions of Christian community today.

Community Prayers

First, the monastic life teaches us about *community prayers.* The monks observe a disciplined rhythm of prayer all day long. These prayer rhythms help each member of the community remain centered on Christ throughout each day. It begins with *Lauds*, a time of prayer before the sun rises in which the monks gather to give thanks to God for the gift of another day. During *Prime* (prayer just before breakfast), the monks call upon the Lord to bless their day and the work of their hands. The offices called *Terce* (9:00 a.m.), *Sext* (noon), and *None* (3:00 p.m.), are brief moments of praise and prayer. They offer tangible occasions to remember one's intention to live with and for the Lord and his Kingdom. *Vespers* are carried out after the day's work is over but just before supper, and includes a longer period of thanksgiving. Then the day ends with *Compline*, a time to reflect on the day, pray prayers of repentance, offer forgiveness, request blessing and protection for the night, and renew one's commitment to live with God when one awakes. Though details may look very different for us, all believers can benefit from following the monks' example of embracing a prayer rhythm throughout each day.

---

[152] M. Basil Pennington, *Lessons From The Monastery That Touch Your Life* (New York: Paulist Press, 1994).

Late Night Watch

Another lesson from the monastery is the discipline of the *late night watch*. Waiting on the Lord in the middle of the night is a way of gaining and regaining spiritual vision and sensitivity. "My soul waits for the Lord more than watchmen wait for the morning" (Psalm 130:6). This discipline of watching and waiting is done in solitude, but is supported by community, for without the encouragement of community, the solitary disciplines are often neglected, losing their significance and relevance to the whole of life.

Encouraging An Abiding Life

The monk's intention in prayer is to call to mind the truth and presence of God, and to support others in that lifestyle. Prayer is the language of grace that enables us to abide with God. I've heard people ask, "How could I ever get anything done if I stopped to pray like the monks?" But this very question betrays that they're missing the point. We are prioritizing fellowship and communion with God and others over productivity—inviting Jesus to be the center of everything we do. Our primary work becomes worshipping and adoring God, and all our other tasks flow from that union—transforming them into acts of worship as well. Surely this speaks of the abundant life that Jesus made possible.

This monastic prayer rhythm is one expression of the apostle Paul's admonition to "pray without ceasing."[153] Every disciple can be challenged and encouraged by the example of regular community gatherings for prayer, which was the pattern of the early church—a pattern we dare not neglect today. The evangelical church must seriously ponder the question, "What is the equivalent means of grace that we are offering our communities to corporately connect with God, and how do we help our members tangibly practice the presence of Christ so they can live the life Jesus made possible?"

---

[153] I Thess. 5:17

No matter how we answer such questions, it is critical to understand that authentic community must be sustained by the living presence of God. "Efforts to organize community artificially can only result in ugly, lifeless caricatures."[154] Structures and programs that give an outward resemblance of Christian community can, in fact, be done apart from the initiative of God, but these configurations can never apprehend all that God has for his people on earth. In fact, artificial community birthed and sustained in the flesh will inevitably become an incubator of unhealthy relationships and spiritual death. A timeless warning against fabricated community is offered by the first generation of Quakers in the late seventeenth century:

> We do not want you to copy or imitate us. We want to be like a ship that has crossed the ocean, leaving a wake of foam, which soon fades away. We want you to follow the Spirit, which we have sought to follow, but which must be sought anew in every generation.[155]

It is critical that every structure and activity of the church be aligned with promoting healthy Christian community. Leaders of spiritual communities must ask, "Why should we add or continue this structure or event? Does it promote fruitful communion, community or mission, or is it just a filler implemented for the sake of activity or attraction?"

CRITICAL ISSUES WITHIN COMMUNITY

The Importance of Solitude

Ironically, healthy cultivation of a spiritual community requires each member to practice solitude with God. When members of a community seek to find in one another what can only be found in God there will be disappointment and dysfunction. We're often tempted to

---

[154] Eberhard Arnold, *Why We Live In Community, with two interpretive talks by Thomas Merton* (Farmington, PA: The Plough Publishing House, 1995), 13.
[155] Arnold, *Why We Live In Community,* iii.

believe that the pain of loneliness will be largely healed through connection to community, but approaching others with this expectation often leads to further pain. After many years of living in, and directing, community life, Jean Vanier tells us:

> We all carry our own deep wound, which is the wound of our loneliness. We find it hard to be alone, and we try to flee from this in hyperactivity, through television and in a million other ways. Some people think their wound of loneliness will be healed if they come into community. But they will be disappointed.[156]

Loneliness will never be eliminated—nor healthy community created—when loneliness reaches out to loneliness. True community is established only when the reality of one person's solitude with God touches that of another. Consider Henri Nouwen's words on the importance of solitude in community:

> Solitude greeting solitude, that's what community is all about. Community is not the place where we are no longer alone but the place where we respect, protect, and reverently greet one another's aloneness. When we allow our aloneness to lead us into solitude, our solitude will enable us to rejoice in the solitude of others. Our solitude roots us in our own hearts. Instead of making us yearn for company that will offer us immediate satisfaction, solitude makes us claim our center and empowers us to call others to claim theirs. Our various solitudes are like strong, straight pillars that hold up the roof of our communal house. Thus, solitude always strengthens community.[157]

---

156 Vanier, *Community and Growth*, 140.
157 Henri J.M. Nouwen, *Bread For The Journey* (San Francisco: HarperCollins, 1997), January 22.

The Means But Not the End

Community is beautiful, but I've observed that its attractiveness can lead us into a serious danger: making community an end in itself rather than a means of grace toward the end, which is communion with God himself. When connecting with others becomes the only goal of community, various forms of relational dysfunction eventually develop. We might call this the 'bad glue' of Christian community. People stick together, but the glue that binds them hinders their wholeness and freedom rather than encouraging it. Examples of this bad relational glue include co-dependence, enmeshment, and control. As Vanier puts it, "We are all so much in need of affection that when somebody gives it to us we want to hold onto it."[158] The primary goals of community are 1) giving glory to Christ, 2) displaying the reality of the good news, and 3) being conformed to his image. As such, the connection between people is meant to be a means of moving us toward realities beyond the relationships themselves. It is imperative that Jesus Christ and his Kingdom remain the central focus and purpose of community. For as Simon Chan warns:

> In the Christian community…Christ stands *between*
> the lovers; union is never direct. No matter how loving
> a relationship, without Christ between the persons in
> love, it threatens to become an idol.[159]

Healthy Christian community is therefore a means of grace that encourages spiritual formation and missional activation. Every serious disciple of Jesus learns that they need to tangibly connect with other disciples in order to support their decision to daily abide under the reign and rule of God.

---

[158] Jean Vanier, *From Brokenness To Community* (New York: Paulist Press, 1992), 37.
[159] Chan, *Spiritual Theology*, 110.

COMMUNITY: THE FELLOWSHIP OF THE IMPERFECT

Critical Components

While there are countless things that could be listed as critical elements to developing a healthy community, the number one factor is the on-going, mutual commitment to cultivating an authentic culture of honor characterized by grace, patience, and truth. The apostle Paul exhorts his readers to "speak the truth in love" (see Ephesians 4:15). We are not meant to convey truth without love, but there also is no authentic Christian love without speaking the truth. Relational health necessitates the tangible existence of both these qualities. Where truth and gracious love are at the heart of community, a safe yet powerful environment arises for growth and healing.

Community can be a wonderful place of encouragement and blessing, "but it is also a place of pain because it will reveal our pride, our fear, and our brokenness."[160] Community can be difficult because we must covenant to remain in relationship with others even when irritation, misunderstandings, and turmoil arise. Where two or more are gathered in Jesus' name, you can count on an eventual relational challenge (it's a good thing Jesus promises to always be with us!). The Bible assumes that we desperately need the Lord and the benefits of the cross to remain in community with other imperfect people— necessitating a lifestyle of forgiving and receiving forgiveness. "Reconciliation is at the heart of community."[161] Believers intending to live life in authentic relationships must also be committed to accepting and respecting differences among one another, allowing diversity to be viewed as a treasure, not a threat. Grace, mercy and patience are not optional for living in community; they are non-negotiables.

---

160 Vanier, *From Brokenness to Community*, 10,11.
161 Vanier, *From Brokenness to Community*, 39.

The Centrality of the Cross

While grace and mercy are rudimentary ingredients that allow real community to thrive, we must expect that Christian community will always be a fellowship of struggling saints. Consider what Dietrich Bonhoeffer says about our attitude toward the reality of sin in the lives of those with whom we are called to live:

> The pious fellowship permits no one to be a sinner. So, everybody must conceal his sin from himself and from the fellowship. We dare not be sinners. Many Christians are unthinkably horrified when a real sinner is suddenly discovered among the righteous. So we remain alone with our sin, living in lies and hypocrisy. The fact is that we *are* sinners![162]

We can only have community with imperfect people, and the illusion of finding a perfect fellowship must be renounced in order for genuine community to be developed. And only God's mercy activated in our hearts makes it possible for our imperfect selves to connect healthily with other imperfect people.

CONCLUSION

The central theme of the Christian message is reconciliation motivated by love. Faith in the Gospel of Jesus establishes people in right relationship with God, and that same Gospel also offers the way to develop right relationships with one another as well. To live in healthy community, we must live together near the cross. The community Jesus calls his disciples to live in will be, by necessity, a miracle of unity in diversity. "It isn't just a question of whether you are building community with people that you naturally like; it is also a question of building community with people that God has brought

---

[162] Dietrich Bonhoeffer, *Life Together* (Harper & Row, 1954), 110.

together."[163] Thus, community requires the exercise of faith in the power of the cross because real problems and differences will certainly manifest. Until we are living together with God in eternity, the only expression of perfect community will be found, "at the intersection of the two segments of the cross, where those who are reconciled with God can be reconciled together."[164] It is only as we realize that we are gifts from God to one another that we will make space for friends who humbly seek to encourage us and hold us lovingly accountable as we journey onward, keeping Jesus as our mutual Center and Source. This is the life that Jesus makes possible!

---

[163] Thomas Merton, as quoted in Eberhard Arnold, *Why We Live In Community*, 51.
[164] Bilezikian, *Community 101*, 35.

FINAL ENCOURAGEMENTS

This book has offered you an invitation to embrace a bigger Gospel. I hope your vision, faith and passion has increased for living the life Jesus made possible. Before I leave you with my final encouragements, let me underscore the highlights of what has been covered through the previous pages.

WHERE WE HAVE BEEN...

In **chapter 1** the meaning and significance of the "good news" as proclaimed by Jesus was clarified. Jesus' revelation did not serve as an introduction of the Kingdom of God, but rather a declaration of the epic news that the reign and rule of God had become accessible through Him in our everyday lives. But while the Kingdom has been *already* at work among us since the first coming of Christ, it does *not yet* have absolute dominion until Christ's return. And so, we live in the tension of a Kingdom that has been inaugurated but not yet consummated. Because the Kingdom has come, we pray with expectation as Jesus taught us, "Thy Kingdom come, Thy will be done on earth as it is in heaven." And often we see some kind of supernatural breakthrough in answer to our prayer, but not always. The only place we will always see the Kingdom have its way is in heaven. And so, we pray, "Let your Kingdom come!"

In **chapter 2** the definition of a disciple and the meaning of discipleship was clarified. We learned that a *disciple* is a follower, student or apprentice of Jesus. A disciple is one who desires to be transformed into the image of Christ, developing His same instinctive responses to the opportunities and challenges of life. *Discipleship* is the intentional lifestyle a disciple engages under the influence of the Holy Spirit to grow in the likeness of Jesus Christ. This is not to be equated with fulfilling a program or curriculum, though it may include that. It is much more. As Jesus put it, "If anyone would come after me (i.e., be my disciple) he must deny himself, take up his cross daily and follow me" (i.e., surrender to a life of discipleship). And so, we pray, "Make me like you, Lord!"

In **chapter 3** we considered God's promise and provision to anoint his followers with his empowering presence. It could not be clearer that God's missional strategy is for his servants to receive power from high to do his Kingdom work on earth. But while every born-again believer has the Spirit resident *within* them, many have not prayed and waited for the Spirit to come *upon* them. Many have been baptized into the body of Christ, while fewer have been baptized by the Spirit with God's power. This situation explains the all too common anemic and fruitless condition of the church today. And so, we pray, "Spirit, anoint us with your empowering presence!"

In **chapter 4** we were reminded that praying for the sick was a core ministry practice of Jesus, and one that he specifically handed off to all those who would follow him. Today the church is often preoccupied with so many things that Jesus never required, while little or no attention is given to his clearest commands. Divine healing can occur when a believer prays for someone's healing with faith and expectation—not faith in faith, but rather faith in the promises and power of God to heal the sick. Such faith is related to our trust that God *can* heal. Expectation relates to our trust that God *will* indeed heal in a specific situation. The disciple's responsibility is not that healing takes place whenever he or she prays for the sick. Rather, it is to be obedient to Scripture and the prompting of the Spirit to be willing to pray for the sick with expectation, while leaving the results in God's hands. Heaven's scorecard calculates our courageous obedience, not our ministry successes or seeming failures. And so, we ask, "May I pray for you?"

In **chapter 5** we celebrated the truth that "God is close to the brokenhearted and saves those crushed in spirit" (Psalm 34:18). In the same way that God can and does heal our physical bodies, he is willing and able to heal and overcome our past pain and failures. Such "inner healing" usually comes more as a progressive unfolding of healing-love and freedom, rather than some sort of quick fix. Learning to apply the cross to the woundings of our inner self is critical to our journey toward holistic health. Mourning our losses, confessing our failures, forgiving those who have offended us, and learning to abide in the truth of who we are and Whose we are, are fundamental disciplines to be exercised in the ministry of inner healing. And so, we pray, "Lord, please heal and transform my wounded soul."

In **chapter 6** we learned that though the devil is a defeated foe, he still can release hellish havoc on earth till Jesus returns and permanently overthrows his reign. Believers are not exempt from being harassed by the demonic realm. Therefore, we must not give the devil a foothold in our lives. Footholds are the landing strips for the enemy. When ministering to the demonized, it is essential to begin with discovering and getting rid of every foothold through confession and renunciation. Once the foothold (or the "right" given to the enemy to be there) has been dealt with, casting out the demon is relatively easy. The church must remain aware that every advance of God's Kingdom is a loss to the enemy's domain, and he won't back down without a fight. Therefore, followers of Jesus must remain vigilant and learn what it means to "put on the full armor of God" (Ephesians 6:13). And so, we pray, "Mighty God, protect us and empower us as we seek to advance your Kingdom over the kingdoms of this world."

In **chapter 7** we discovered that the term "Spiritual formation" is simply describing a disciple's lifestyle of making space for God. While the promise that the disciple who abides will automatically bear much fruit (John 15:5), no one automatically abides. We must give intention and effort to making space in our lives for this to be a reality. This underscores the purpose and importance of the spiritual disciplines. Practicing any spiritual discipline must not be viewed as an end in itself, but rather a means to cultivate focus and movement toward abiding with God everywhere and always. Following the example of Jesus and the fruitful ones that have gone before us, it is beneficial to begin one's day in the presence of God. The purpose is to align one's heart and mind on the truth of who we are and Whose we are. Then, as we rise to engage the day before us, we allow our established "remembrances" to keep us awake to the reality that the all-powerful God who loves us, is always with us everywhere. And so, we pray, "Grace me this day to remain awake to your abiding presence."

In **chapter 8** we concluded with an emphasis on the essential contribution intentional community plays in living the life Jesus made possible. The isolated disciple has no chance of establishing and sustaining a fruitful life. Everyone needs to be authentically connected to some supportive friends who will tangibly encourage and hold them accountable on life's journey. Such friends make themselves available and vulnerable to one another. While the cry for community is encoded in our soul by the finger of God, many give great effort to avoid such connection. Why? For fear of being wounded again and again. Failure to face and overcome this fear, is a failure to love and be loved. In the community of the King, disciples must learn to plant the cross again and again in the middle of every relationship. And so, we pray, "Lord, grace me to forgive and love others as you have forgiven and loved me."

WHERE DO WE GO FROM HERE?

What is most needed to ignite our life trajectory toward flourishing? I am certain it is not to be found in reading one more book, running to the latest seminar, or listening to yet another inspirational podcast. While any of these can play a role in our development, what is most needed for most of us is a large dose of courageous obedience. The reason for this is that what we mentally grasp does not by itself unleash the transformation and growth needed to cultivate a fruitful life. It is what we do with what we learn that has the capacity to bring about revolutionary change. The apostle Paul hammers this truth home when he writes; "Whatever you have learned or received or heard from me, or seen in me–*put it into practice*. And the God of peace with be with you" (Philip 4:9, emphasis added). The urgent needs of our broken world will never be met by believers committed only to *learning* more about God, discipleship, spiritual formation, healing or deliverance. We have been commissioned to tangibly abide with God, make disciples, pray for the sick and set the captives free. Every disciple is meant to be able and ready to *do such things* within the context of their everyday lives.

Further, our clear mandate was not first to *improve* the quality of disciples and churches, but to *multiply* them. My challenge to you is to take what you have learned in this book, apply it to your own life, but then go and give it all away to others as the Spirit leads you. Live it, give it and raise up many others who will do the same. Here are some ideas for how you might go about doing this:

- Gather weekly with a few friends who will commit to read through the book with the intention of experimenting with the content of each chapter. The group could agree to read a specific chapter, then come together to discuss it, followed by each person stating at least one way they will seek to put the content into practice. The next meeting should begin with sharing about the activation experiment.

- A church leadership team could follow this same strategy, but perhaps include some time to discuss how they might integrate their discoveries in the context of their ministry.

- Church planters could complement the focus of their strategic efforts with the challenging themes of this book. How awesome to have the life Jesus made possible accessible at the foundation of a new work!

- Ministry coaches and Spiritual directors could selectively use the material in this book to help prepare for or follow up on a conversation that touches on a related theme. I know firsthand that the themes covered in this book surface often in the context of coaching others.

Lastly, I want to encourage you to remember the promise of God, that his presence will always be with you everywhere. I find it both significant and strategic that Jesus makes this promise directly after speaking the great commission, "Go and make disciples...teaching them to obey everything I have commanded you. And surely I am with you always, to the very end of the age" (Matt 28:18-20). So be courageously obedient my friend. We don't go after any of this alone!

It's now time to live the life Jesus made possible.

ABOUT THE AUTHOR

Bill Randall serves on staff with Church Resource Ministries (CRM), a missional agency that works to create movements of committed followers of Jesus throughout the world (www.crmleaders.org). He is the founding Director of Pioneering Initiatives. In this role, Bill leads a strategic ministry designed to provide training, holistic coaching and resources to leaders and teams serving around the world committed to pioneering new expressions of church that result from making more and better disciples of Jesus from among the harvest (www.PioneeringInitiatives.org). Bill has an earned doctorate from Fuller Theological Seminary.

Prior to serving as the Director of Pioneering Initiatives with CRM, Bill served as a church planter, local church lead pastor, University and Seminary professor, conference speaker and retreat facilitator. Bill and his wife Jill have ministered closely together throughout their married lives. Jill currently serves as the Director of Staff Vitality for ChurchNEXT/CRM. Bill and Jill have three married children and five grandchildren and live within a few miles of their whole clan in Nampa, Idaho.

WHAT IS PIONEERING INITIATIVES?

Pioneering Initiatives is a collection of leaders and teams situated around the world committed to making disciples from among the harvest, developing emerging leaders, multiplying everything, with the celebrated outcome of new expressions of multiplying churches. Our priorities and values include:

- We prioritize the *multiplication* of Jesus-followers from among the harvest rather than simply *improving* aspects of the existing church.

- Pioneering Initiatives begins with disciple-making and leadership development from among the harvest as opposed to prioritizing the launching of a new ministry venue.

- Pioneering Initiatives appreciates the fact that for a person to make disciples of not-yet-believers, one has to first become friends with not-yet-believers.

- Pioneering Initiatives utilizes discovery-based learning rather than expert dependent ministry execution.

- With Pioneering Initiatives, new expressions of church are launched by an apostolic missionary team, rather than a church planter who will assume primary leadership of the new church as it develops. From the very beginning, the apostolic missionary team will limit the amount of time they lead from "the middle of the room". As people wired as shepherd/teacher are discovered, they are trained and released to lead from the middle, while the apostolic team leads increasingly from behind.

- Pioneering Initiatives functionally embraces the Ephesians 4 Five-Fold Ascension Gift typology for leadership and ministry execution throughout all aspects of the missional initiative. This is essential if the hope of *launching* and *sustaining* gospel movements is to become a reality. The following summary is taken from J.R. Woodward, *The Church as Movement*:

  - Apostles – Catalyze & co-mission (Dream awakeners)
  - Prophets – Expose & embody (Heart revealers)
  - Evangelists – Invite & excite (Story tellers)
  - Shepherds – Guard & guide (Soul healers)
  - Teachers – Interpret & inform (Light givers)

- The Pioneering Initiatives teams consider supernatural ministry a priority, and a normal means of revealing the gospel and developing disciples. This is one very important way we follow the example and instruction of Jesus. Our ambition is not to be "charismatic" (as some understand it), but rather, to be like Jesus in word and deed.

  - The Holy Spirit *in* us – Regeneration
  - The Holy Spirit *on* us – Anointing
  - The Holy Spirit *through* us - Ministry

- Pioneering Initiatives uses a unique scorecard to evaluate success:

- Advancing the Kingdom **vs** measuring institutional growth

- Multiplication **vs** simply improving disciples and churches. This necessitates that our model remains simple (not easy), inexpensive and can be replicated at every level.

- How many are participating and being transformed **vs** counting how many are gathering to consume.

- How many are obeying the Word **vs** how many are simply learning the content of the Word.

COULD PIONEERING INITIATIVES BE A FIT FOR YOU?

If you are a Kingdom focused leader and find yourself often frustrated with the Sunday/facility centric, consumer driven version of church that is all too common in today's world, it might be worthwhile for you to consider if you have been wired by God to serve as an apostolic missionary. There are few things more confusing and frustrating than trying to flourish as an apostolically wired leader while serving in a non-apostolic ministry context. It feels like you are bumping up against a powerful machine that is designed to marginalize rather than appreciate your God given ministry instincts.

Pioneering Initiatives missionaries are consumed with multiplying disciples from among the harvest rather than simply improving the existing church. At the same time we deeply appreciate the strategic role that the local church plays in maturing and sustaining the harvest. New expressions of culturally relevant local churches are the intentional outcome of our pioneering efforts. We are also convinced that the local church is meant to be the body of Christ on mission in a specific geographical context. But such Kingdom outposts must be consistently informed, influenced and networked with apostolically gifted leaders to resist the monumental historical drift toward missional irrelevancy.

If this line of thought catches your attention, please get in touch with us. We'd love to connect with you, hear your story and begin a prayerful discernment process to see if your calling and wiring are a fit with Pioneering Initiatives.

You can contact us from our website at:
www.PioneeringInitiatives.org.

Made in the USA
Las Vegas, NV
28 September 2021

31307656R00132